Cohesion Policy and Multi-level Governance in South East Europe

I0129478

This book considers the extent to which EU cohesion policy and related pre-accession instruments are contributing to the development of more compound polities in south east Europe and, specifically, promoting multi-level governance. In this respect, there are two points of departure: the first is the argument that the EU is a highly compound polity that tends to pull member (and candidate) states in this direction; the second is the considerable literature that links EU cohesion policy to the promotion of multi-level governance. Following this, we have chosen a range of south east European states whose period of engagement with the EU generally differs: Greece, Slovenia, Bulgaria, Romania, Croatia, F.Y.R. Macedonia and Turkey. The case studies reveal that EU cohesion policy has created more compound polities but that system-wide multi-level governance remains weak and central governments are still prominent. However, there are interesting and potentially important developments in relation to particular features of multi-level governance, not least in states whose engagement with the EU in this sphere is relatively new.

This book was published as a special issue of *Southeast European and Black Sea Studies*.

Ian Bache is Professor of Politics at the University of Sheffield. His books include Europeanization and Multi-level Governance: Cohesion Policy in the European Union and Britain (2008), Politics in the European Union (2006, with Stephen George), The Europeanization of British Politics (2006, with Andrew Jordan) and Multi-level Governance (2004, with Matthew Flinders).

George Andreou is elected Lecturer at the Aristotle University of Thessaloniki. He has published the book *The New Cohesion Policy of the EU and Greece* (in Greek) (2007, with P. Liargovas).

Cohesion Policy and Multi-level Governance in South East Europe

Edited by
Ian Bache and George Andreou

Routledge
Taylor & Francis Group

LONDON AND NEW YORK

First published 2011
by Routledge
2 Park Square, Milton Park, Abingdon, Oxon, OX14 4RN

Simultaneously published in the USA and Canada
by Routledge
711 Third Avenue, New York, NY 10017

Routledge is an imprint of the Taylor & Francis Group, an informa business

© 2011 Taylor & Francis

First issued in paperback 2013

This book is a reproduction of *Southeast Europe and Black Sea Studies*, vol.10, issue 1. The Publisher requests to those authors who may be citing this book to state, also, the bibliographical details of the special issue on which the book was based.

Typeset in Times by Taylor & Francis Books

British Library Cataloguing in Publication Data
A catalogue record for this book is available from the British Library

ISBN13: 978-0-415-59419-6 (hbk)

ISBN13: 978-0-415-85284-5 (pbk)

Disclaimer
The publisher would like to make readers aware that the chapters in this book are referred to as articles as they had been in the special issue. The publisher accepts responsibility for any inconsistencies that may have arisen in the course of preparing this volume for print.

Contents

Europeanization and multi-level governance: EU cohesion policy and pre-accession aid in Southeast Europe

Ian Bache

Department of Politics, University of Sheffield, Sheffield, UK

This opening contribution provides the framework for discussion for the case studies that follow. It outlines the key concepts employed – simple and compound polities, Europeanization and multi-level governance – and explains the origins and development of EU cohesion policy and related pre-accession instruments. It concludes by summarizing the main themes and issues addressed in the subsequent contributions.

Introduction

This volume considers the extent to which EU cohesion policy and related pre-accession instruments are contributing to the development of more compound polities in Southeast Europe and, specifically, promoting multi-level governance. In light of previous research (below), we anticipate variations in the nature and extent of EU pressures and incentives over time both across and even within states. Following this, we have chosen for this study a range of Southeast European states whose period of engagement with the EU generally differs: Greece (George Andreou) has been a member of the EU throughout the period under observation (1989–2008); Slovenia (George Andreou and Ian Bache) joined as part of the 2004 enlargement; Bulgaria (Alexander Yanakiev) and Romania (Ana Maria Dobre) acceded to the EU in 2007; Croatia (Ian Bache and Danijel Tomšić) is expected to join in the near future; and F.Y.R. Macedonia (Gorica Atanasova and Ian Bache) and Turkey (Ebru Ertugal) have a longer-term prospect of membership. In Schmidt's (2006) terms, each of these countries would be characterized as a 'simple polity' and, as such, particularly susceptible to pressure for change through engaging with the highly compound EU polity. We begin the discussion by explaining the conceptual themes employed throughout the volume.

Conceptual themes

The simple–compound polity distinction and multi-level governance

In essence, simple polities are characterized by power and influence being concentrated in a single level and mode of governance, whereas compound polities are characterized

1

by multiple levels and modes of governance. More specifically, the term 'simple polity' refers to a state with a combination of a majoritarian system of representation, statist policy-making processes and a unitary state structure. The term 'compound polity' refers to a state with a combination of a proportional representation system, corporatist policy-making processes and regionalized or federalized structures (Schmidt 2006, 227).

Using these categories, the EU is defined as a *highly compound* regional polity, which places it at the extreme end of the continuum that includes its member states and one that tends to pull all member states – irrespective of their place on the continuum – in this direction. However, the pressure on states furthest away from the EU on this continuum is likely to be comparatively greater:

> The EU's federalizing effects undermine the traditional concentration of power of the unitary structures of simple polities while it challenges organizing principles which assume that democracy is better served by the concentration of governmental power and authority, such that the government has the sole responsibility as well as the capacity to respond to citizens' wants and needs effectively 'for the people'. (Schmidt 2006, 34)

In a similar way, while the EU tends to 'pluralize' all member states' policy-making processes by promoting the role of organized interests in policy-making, it is seen to have had a greater impact in those states where interests tend to have been relatively excluded (Schmidt 2006, 34–5).

Schmidt's emphasis on the 'federalizing' (also 'regionalizing' elsewhere in her discussion) and 'pluralizing' effects relates directly to the notion of multi-level governance, which refers to increasingly complex vertical relations between actors organized at various territorial levels and horizontal relations between actors from public, private and voluntary spheres. It is a process of change characterized by the emergence of 'territorially overarching policy networks' (Marks 1993, 402–3) and one that challenges the role, power and authority of national governments. Moreover, referring to specific types of multi-level governance developed in the literature refines our focus here. Type I multi-level governance describes system-wide governing arrangements in which the dispersion of authority is restricted to a limited number of clearly defined, non-overlapping jurisdictions at a limited number of territorial levels, each of which has responsibility for a 'bundle' of functions. By contrast, Type II multi-level governance describes governing arrangements in which the jurisdiction of authority is task-specific, where jurisdictions operate at numerous territorial levels and may be overlapping (Marks and Hooghe 2004). In Type I, authority is relatively stable, but in Type II it is more flexible to deal with the changing demands of governance (Table 1). Type I and Type II multi-level governance typically co-exist in modern polities.

In relation to Schmidt's categories of simple and compound polities, Type I governance relates to the dimension of state structures, whereas Type II governance relates to the nature of policy-making processes (pluralist or statist). Here, we are examining

Table 1. Types of multi-level governance.

Type I	Type II
General-purpose jurisdictions	Task-specific jurisdictions
Non-intersecting memberships	Intersecting memberships
Jurisdictions at a limited number of levels	No limit to the number of jurisdictional levels
System-wide architecture	Flexible design

Source: Marks and Hooghe (2004, 17).

the extent to which Type I governance has been changed through greater regionalization of state structures and the extent to which Type II governance has been enhanced to promote pluralization of policy-making processes. In clarifying the relationship between these concepts in this way, we are able to relate our findings to two related bodies of work that are generally treated separately.

Europeanization

While the term 'Europeanization' has been used in a number of ways (see Olsen 2002), it is employed here in its most prominent usage to refer to the effects of the EU on domestic politics. Specifically, Europeanization is understood as 'the reorientation or reshaping of politics (and governance) in the domestic arena in ways that reflect policies, practices or preferences advanced through the EU system of governance' (Bache and Jordan 2006, 30). It is an approach that emphasizes both the need to understand what is 'coming down' from the EU (e.g. the nature and the force of a particular instrument) and how this 'fits' with and is mediated by domestic circumstances. In principle, the greater the degree of misfit between the EU requirements and the domestic circumstances, the greater the adaptational pressures. However, a range of domestic responses are possible, leading to varying degrees of domestic change (see Börzel and Risse 2003, 69–70; Bache 2008, 12).

Central to much of the Europeanization literature are the insights of the new institutionalisms and, in particular, the contrasting claims of rational, sociological and historical variants. The first two provide the contrasting claims of the logic of consequentiality versus the logic of appropriateness (Börzel and Risse 2003). The former emphasizes rational goal-driven action whereby actors readjust their strategies to achieve unchanged goals in a new context, whereas the latter refers to a more complex process of social learning in which actors' goals or preferences are changed. Although, as March and Olsen (1998, 10) have argued, 'any particular action probably involves elements of each'.

An appreciation of the new institutionalisms is helpful in understanding the relationship between Europeanization and multi-level governance through EU cohesion policy and pre-accession aid. Here, Thielemann's (1999) work is particularly instructive because it sets out two positions on the implications for European governance of the partnership principle of EU cohesion policy (below) and links the rationalist–sociological debate with the discussion of policy networks, which is closely associated with the concept of multi-level governance (see Bache 2008, 21–38).

In this debate, there are two main views. The first position, linked to the Rhodes (1988, 1997) model of policy networks, is underpinned by the rationalist/consequentialist logic and emphasizes partnership as a mechanism for creating new opportunities for strategic interaction. In this view, power is zero-sum and Europeanization results from a redistribution of power resources between actors in the domestic arena as a result of engaging with the EU. The second position, most closely associated with Kohler-Koch (1996) and her collaborators, suggests that network governance provides the potential for a deeper transformation of actor behaviour and preferences. In this view, the regular interaction promoted by the partnership principle can generate trust through socialization that promotes problem-solving rather than bargaining as the predominant decision-making style (Thielemann 1999, 187–8).

Here can be seen a clear contrast between rationalist and sociological strands in parallel debates on new institutionalism and policy networks, which generate

Table 2.   Rationalist and sociological assumptions underpinning Europeanization research.

Assumptions	Rationalist accounts	Sociological accounts
Power	Zero-sum	Positive-sum
Interests	Fixed	Malleable
Mechanism of Europeanization	Redistribution of power resources	Socialization/learning

Source: Adapted from Bache (2008, 13).

contrasting hypotheses in relation to the nature and the extent of the transformation of governance that has taken place through EU cohesion policy. A rationalist account would assume power to be zero-sum, expect national actors to continue pursuing established goals (albeit in a changing environment) and ascribe shifts toward multi-level governance to a redistribution of power resources brought by the EU policies. By contrast, a sociological perspective would assume power to be positive-sum, expect actors to change their preferences through socialization in a changing environment and ascribe shifts toward multi-level governance to a learning process (see Table 2).

In both accounts, learning is seen to be a feature of change, but has a different meaning in each. The central distinction is between 'thin' (or single loop) and 'thick' (or double loop) forms of learning (Radaelli 2003, 52). 'Thin learning' refers to the readjustment of actor strategies to allow them to achieve unchanged goals in a new context or 'how to get around an obstacle by using a menu of well-known responses in various ingenious ways' (Radaelli 2003, 38). 'Thick learning' involves a modification of actors' values and thus a reshaping of their preferences and goals.

So far, this rationalist–reflectivist dichotomy is relatively straightforward, but does not account for historical institutionalism, a key component in Europeanization research (Bulmer and Radaelli 2005; Bulmer and Burch 2006). As an approach, it incorporates both rationalist and sociological elements, but emphasizes the importance of practices embedded over time in explaining how institutions respond to external pressures for change. More broadly, it relates to questions of time and timing – and particularly the argument that '*when* things happen within a sequence affects *how* they happen' (Tilly 1984, 14) – that deserve attention here, given the focus on states whose engagement with the EU varies across these dimensions.

Pierson (2004) makes a persuasive case for research going beyond snapshots of political life to analysis of 'moving pictures' that situate politics more squarely in time. At the core of this approach is not only that 'history matters' in explaining contemporary political phenomena, but also the need to explore how and with what effects. The approach emphasizes the importance of path dependence, highlighting the importance of self-reinforcing or positive feedback processes that constrain change. Thus, historical institutionalism is often most useful in explaining outcomes approximating inertia or incremental change. However, the approach anticipates occasional sudden change through 'seismic events that trigger a "critical juncture" or "punctuate" the pre-existing equilibrium' (Bulmer 2007, 50).

In the context of Europeanization research, the history that matters is both that of the EU and of the member or candidate country under consideration. Thus, the research task is to understand something of both, but also the relationship between them as they intertwine and exert mutual influence. The point at which they interact is important in shaping the nature of their interaction. As Pierson (2004) puts it: 'Just as a falling brick has distinct consequences when it arrives at the same time as an unfortunate pedestrian, the simultaneity of two processes that in other cases occur at different times produces critical consequences' (12). Part of this comparative endeavour is to explore the importance of the different historical paths trodden by our case study countries for mediating Europeanization pressures.

In short, the concept of Europeanization highlights the importance of the nature, precision and status of EU requirements and their goodness of fit with member/applicant states; emphasizes the potential importance of both processes involving repeated interactions between the EU and individual states as well as a top-down process of change; demands a focus on the domestic circumstances that may constrain or facilitate change; and provides categorizations to capture the extent of the change that has (or has not) taken place. And finally, it is a concept that increasingly models for research questions exploring the possibility of other supra/international sources of domestic change, as well as domestic sources, to avoid the over-attribution of change to EU effects (see Bache 2008, 15–19).

Where the concept of Europeanization has been applied to either studies of candidate states (e.g. Schimmelfennig and Sedelmeier 2005) or to studies of cohesion policy (e.g. Andreou 2006; Bache 2008) or indeed to both at the same time (e.g. Hughes, Sasse, and Gordon 2004, 2005), rationalist explanations for domestic change have been prominent: actors have revised domestic practices primarily to comply with either membership conditionality, the *acquis*, or to receive funding. However, some studies have indicated the possibility of social learning through long-term engagement with EU cohesion policy (e.g. Bache 2008), whereas others have highlighted a less profound but still significant *policy* learning, in which actors draw lessons from EU practices but without altering their core goals or preferences (e.g. Paraskevopoulos 2006).

Hypotheses and questions

Based on Schmidt's work and on the cohesion policy literature, we hypothesize that EU cohesion policy and related pre-accession aid requirements are likely to pull our case study states in a more compound direction. Beyond testing this hypothesis, our purpose here is also to consider specifically whether Europeanization is having effects on the system-wide architecture of the case study states (in particular through regionalization), on the proliferation of pluralistic processes (especially through partnership) or in promoting task-specific governance arrangements. The contributors draw on the insights of the new institutionalisms to explain developments.

Cohesion policy and related pre-accession aid

EU cohesion policy refers to a range of financial instruments aimed at addressing economic and social disparities in Europe. Most obviously, this covers the structural funds, which are aimed at member states. However, a number of related pre-accession instruments prepare the ground for structural funding post-accession. As will become clear, there are some differences in the governing principles of different instruments, but also some common features. Moreover, over time there are variations in how the European Commission has interpreted some principles over time.

Cohesion policy was given a treaty base for the first time in the Single European Act (1987). The subsequent reform of the structural funds that came into effect in

1989 brought the European Regional Development Fund (ERDF), European Social Fund (ESF) and the guidance section of the European Agricultural Guarantee and Guidance Fund (EAGGF) into a common policy framework and led to a doubling of financial allocations by 1993. The key components of this policy framework have remained largely intact ever since.

The reformed policy had a strong regional focus, which required the EU to adopt a system for classifying its territorial units below the national level. It did this by adopting the NUTS[1] system, which provided a hierarchical categorization of different territorial units in the EU according to five levels, the largest being NUTS 1 (sections of a country grouping together basic regions). This level was subdivided into NUTS 2 (basic regions), with subdivisions continuing through NUTS 3 and NUTS 4 to the smallest level of NUTS 5 (villages and towns). NUTS 2 regions, which were generally defined by member states for their own regional policy purposes, were the ones adopted for the main territorial objectives of cohesion policy.[2] For practical reasons – i.e. the availability of suitable data – the NUTS categories were generally based on the existing institutional divisions within member states.[3]

The doubling of financial allocations for the structural funds in this reform was accompanied by important policy revisions: *concentration* focused funds on areas of greatest need, *programming* required regions to develop strategic multi-annual plans to ensure coherence between projects funded and *partnership* required that funds be administered through regional partnerships within each state, consisting of representatives of national government, regional (or local) government and the European Commission. Following the principle of concentration, structural fund expenditure was focused on five objectives, three with an explicit regional dimension (Objectives 1, 2 and 5b). The bulk of spending was focused on the most disadvantaged regions eligible under Objective 1 (approximately 65% of total structural fund allocations).[4]

In 1991, the Cohesion Fund was created to assist member states with a GDP of less than 90% of the Community average. This was not part of cohesion policy until 2007 and until then not governed by the same principles: there was no regional breakdown of funding; funding was allocated to individual projects rather than to multi-project programmes; and the partnership and additionality requirements were more relaxed.

The cohesion policy principles agreed in 1988 were maintained in the 1993 reform and also in 1999, when the focus of reform was on preparing the ground for the accession of Central and Eastern European (CEE) countries with an average GDP of typically around one-third of the EU average. In 1999, in preparation for enlargement to include countries with an average GDP of typically around one-third of the EU average, a number of new instruments were introduced. The Instrument for Structural Policies for Pre-Accession (ISPA) provided funding for environment and transport projects as a forerunner to Cohesion Fund allocations; the Phare programme (Poland and Hungary: Aid for Economic Restructuring)[5] aimed to strengthen economic and social cohesion and develop administrative and institutional capacity in anticipation of structural funds, whereas Special Accession Programme for Agricultural and Rural Development (Sapard) played a similar role for rural areas.

In January 2007, a single Instrument for Pre-Accession Assistance (IPA) came into effect, which replaced the instruments introduced for the 2000–2006 period. IPA covers the candidate states (Croatia, F.Y.R. Macedonia, Turkey) and the potential candidate states (Albania, Bosnia and Herzegovina, Montenegro, Serbia – including Kosovo) and has five components: (1) transition assistance and institution building,

(2) cross-border cooperation, (3) regional development, (4) human resources development, and (5) rural development (DG Enlargement 2007, 1).

The implications for domestic governance

Three principles of cohesion policy that were introduced in 1989 require compound polity characteristics to be developed in recipient states where they do not already exist and thus have direct relevance for research on Europeanization and multi-level governance. These are the principles of regionalization, partnership and programming; the first of which relates to the vertical dimension of multi-level governance, whereas the latter two have both vertical and horizontal implications.

Regionalization requires that funds be administered at regional level within states, usually at the NUTS 2 level. This focus led to both the adoption of the NUTS classification of territorial units below the national level in each member state and the involvement of subnational actors in the policy-making process through regional programming undertaken by regional partnerships. The nature of the main territorial objectives (1 and 2) of the structural funds remained largely unchanged until 2006, with the changes that occurred not affecting the focus of the research presented here.[6] Moreover, the proportions of the EU population covered by these objectives remained relatively consistent up to 2006 (see Leonardi 2005, 16). In 2006, the structural fund objectives were renamed and somewhat redefined.[7]

Partnership requires funds to be administered by actors from different organizations working together. Initially, this principle focused on promoting interaction between governmental actors from different levels, but has increasingly placed greater emphasis on engaging non-state actors (see Bache 2010) and thus has both vertical and horizontal dimensions.

Programming effectively commits actors to work together in partnership for a sustained period of time (between three and seven years) in developing and implementing regional strategies. The switch to multi-annual programming in 1989 drew on the experience of experiments piloted in Greece in the mid-1980s through the Integrated Mediterranean Programmes (see Andreou 2010). Programming was not just multi-annual, but also sought to integrate the different structural funding instruments operating in different sectors.

The pre-accession instruments have not been governed by these principles of cohesion policy and until relatively recently did not have significant implications for multi-level governance. However, the IPA introduced in 2007 has features that deliberately mimic cohesion policy requirements to prepare candidate countries more effectively for managing cohesion policy post-accession – a development that was triggered by the lack of preparedness of some of the 2004 entrants. These changes have enhanced the prospects for pre-accession aid promoting multi-level governance. Within the European Commission, DG Regio has traditionally had responsibility for cohesion policy, whereas DG Enlargement has administered pre-accession aid. However, under IPA, DG Regio has responsibility for those components (3 and 4) that mimic cohesion policy requirements, although DG Enlargement retains overall responsibility for the coordination of pre-accession aid. Whereas Components 3 and 4 of IPA aim specifically at preparing states for managing the structural funds post-accession, the emphasis within Component 1 on developing civil society relates directly to Components 3 and 4 and to the horizontal dimension of multi-level governance specifically. Table 3 summarizes the key requirements of

Table 3. Key requirements of cohesion policy and pre-accession instruments with implications for multi-level governance.

Cohesion instrument	Key requirements	Case study coverage
Main structural funds (ERDF, ESF, EAGGF)	Partnership, programming and regionalization	Greece (1989–present) Slovenia (2004–present) Bulgaria (2007–present) Romania (2007–present)
Integrated Mediterranean Programmes (IMPs)	Partnership and programming	Greece (1985–1992)
Cohesion Fund	Partnership	Greece (1994–present) Slovenia (2004–present) Bulgaria (2007–present) Romania (2007–present)
Pre-accession instruments (Phare/ Obnova, Sapard, ISPA)	Decentralization	Slovenia (1992–2003) Croatia (2004–2006) F.Y.R. Macedonia (1996–2006) Bulgaria (1990–2006) Romania (1990–2006)
EDIS	Decentralization	Slovenia (2004–2006)
CARDS	Decentralization	Croatia (2005–present) F.Y.R. Macedonia (2005–present)
IPA	Decentralization, partnership and programming	Croatia (2007–present) F.Y.R. Macedonia (2007–present) Turkey (2007–present)
MEDA	Partnership and programming	Turkey (1996–2001)
Pre-accession instrument for Turkey	Decentralization	Turkey (2002–2006)

cohesion policy and various pre-accession instruments with implications for multi-level governance.

Existing studies

There have been a number of studies that have reflected on the extent to which EU cohesion policy has promoted multi-level governance. Hooghe's (1996) collection on the implementation of cohesion policy across the EU15 focused on the effects on territorial relations. It found considerable variation in the degree of multi-level governance evident, not only in different states, but also in different regions within the same state. Here, a central explanation was the importance of pre-existing pattern of territorial relations within states: in particular, governments in centralized states could be effective gatekeepers in controlling the domestic flow of EU resources and rendering the multi-level structures and processes established as a condition of funding largely symbolic. Later research funded by the European Commission (Tavistock Institute 1999) confirmed this pattern of differentiated multi-level governance emerging through EU cohesion policy.

Studies of CEE countries in their accession period have paid close attention to the role of the Commission in advancing multi-level governance. These studies suggest that while the Commission initially sought to advance regionalization in CEE countries, inspired by ideals of multi-level governance, as accession grew closer its position shifted to ensuring that the funds were absorbed on time, even if this meant they were managed centrally through national ministries (Marcou 2002, 25; Leonardi 2005, 164). Bailey and De Propris's (2002) study of the Czech Republic, Estonia, Hungary, Poland and Slovenia identified national government 'gatekeepers' 'firmly in control' of subnational actors, who were able to participate in but not significantly influence the policy process. Hughes, Sasse, and Gordon's (2004, 2005) research on Estonia, Hungary, Poland and Slovenia emphasized the importance of historical institutional traditions in each state in shaping the degree of regionalization emerging, echoing the findings of the earlier research on the EU15.

Two more recent studies provide a mixed picture of the impact of cohesion policy on regionalization in the Central and East European states. Bachtler and McMaster (2008) identify 'several points to support the contention that the role of regions has increased in terms of their legitimacy, institutional capacity and stability' (420) but also suggest that 'the limitations and barriers to regional participation in the funds currently outweigh the opportunities' (421). Their bottom line is to challenge the idea that structural funds necessarily lead to stronger regions. Bruszt (2008) explains how the Commission's turn to (re)centralization for administering funds in the pre-accession period was resisted in some states and thus features of multi-level governance emerged. Here, the governance changes are explained in historical institutionalist terms as 'layering': 'the emergence of change on the margins, implying local rule transformation within a basically unchanged institution that does not challenge the dominant characteristics of the mode of governance' (Bruszt 2008, 620).

The study by Bache (2008) of the EU25 considers the impact of cohesion policy on Type I and Type II multi-level governance. It identifies a trend toward multi-level governance across Europe, although this remains uneven. Moreover, while this trend is not due primarily to states' engagement with the EU, it is not possible to understand the nature and pace of the changes evident without reference to the EU and its cohesion policy. However, the effects of EU cohesion policy have been more pronounced on Type II multi-level governance than on Type I, with ad hoc functionally-specific governance arrangements emerging at various territorial levels as a direct response.

In all cases of research in this field, the devil was often to be found in the domestic detail rather than in the letter of the EU's requirements. Our purpose here is to explore these domestic details in a new comparative context, focusing on a particular region of Europe, drawing on some new cases and new empirical data.

Conclusion

To summarize, the purpose of this volume is to consider the extent to which EU cohesion policy and related pre-accession instruments are contributing to the development of more compound polities in Southeast Europe and, specifically, promoting multi-level governance. In this respect, the discussion has two points of departure: the first is the argument by Schmidt (2006) that the EU is a highly compound polity that tends to pull member states in this direction; the second is the considerable literature that links EU cohesion policy to the promotion of multi-level governance. In addressing the core questions, contributors are encouraged to draw on the new institutionalist strand of the Europeanization literature that offers insights into the domestic responses to EU incentives and pressures.

The case studies that follow adopt a similar format. Each one begins with a brief background on the nature of governance and politics in the country studied before providing an overview of the cohesion policy and related pre-accession instruments that have operated there. The presentation of the main findings considers the extent to which these have contributed to the development of a more compound polity and, specifically, to the promotion of multi-level governance. While we ask the authors to reflect on both types of multi-level governance, it is clear from the existing studies that significant effects on Type I are far less likely than on Type II.

In addition, the authors are asked to consider any other important effects that the EU's cohesion policy and related instruments have had on domestic governance and politics and, specifically, to reflect on the implications for the role, power and authority of the central state in the domestic context. In engaging with the Europeanization literature, contributors are asked to explicitly consider the importance of non-EU explanations for change, whether from domestic or international sources.

The concluding contribution of the collection draws comparative insights and reflects on the extent to which multi-level governance is being built in Southeast Europe and whether this should be understood as a feature of Europeanization.

Acknowledgements

I would like to thank my co-editor George Andreou and the two anonymous referees for the journal for their helpful comments. All the usual disclaimers apply.

Notes

1. Nomenclature of Territorial Units for Statistics. The NUTS acronym originated from the French *nomenclature des unités territoriales statistiques*.
2. NUTS 2 for defining Objective 1 regions, but NUTS 3 for defining Objective 2 regions.
3. From 2004 the NUTS nomenclature was extended to the new member states, which meant that on 1 May 2004 the territory of the EU was subdivided into 89 regions at NUTS 1 level, 254 regions at NUTS 2 level and 1214 regions at NUTS 3 level. NUTS 4 became Local Administrative Units (LAU) 1 and NUTS 5 became LAU 2.
4. The objectives were as follows – Objective 1: Promoting the development of 'less developed regions', that is, those with per capita GDP of less than 75% of the Community average, or just above this figure under 'special circumstances' (ERDF, ESF and EAGGF – Guidance section); Objective 2: Converting the regions seriously affected by industrial decline (ERDF and ESF); Objective 3: Combating long-term unemployment: assisting people aged over 25, unemployed for over a year (ESF); Objective 4: Assisting the occupational integration of young people, that is, people below the age of 25 (ESF); Objective 5: (a) Accelerating the adjustment of agricultural structures (EAGGF – Guidance section), and (b) promoting the development of rural areas (EAGGF – Guidance section, ESF, ERDF). In addition to the 'mainstream' structural funds allocated according to the five objectives, approximately 9% of the ERDF budget was retained for 'Community Initiatives'. These were programmes devised by the Commission to meet outstanding regional needs.
5. Phare was subsequently extended to other accession states.
6. In 1993 reform, Objectives 1 and 2 were not changed from 1988, but Objectives 3 and 4 were merged to create a new Objective 3. This new Objective 3 was aimed at 'facilitating the integration … of those threatened with exclusion from the labour market' (European Commission 1993, 11). A new Objective 4 was designed to give effect to new tasks laid down in the Maastricht Treaty to 'facilitate workers' adaptation to industrial changes and to changes in production systems' (European Commission 1993, 11). Objective 5a maintained its initial goal of accelerating the adjustment of agricultural structures as part of the CAP reform, but a new fund was added to assist the fisheries: the Financial Instrument of Fisheries Guidance (FIFG). Problems arising from the decline in fishing and fish-processing activities would also be addressed through Objectives 1, 2 and 5b. Objective 5b changed slightly from the 'development of rural areas' to the 'development and structural adjustment of rural areas' (European Commission 1993, 11). Objective 6 status was created

to provide assistance to the sparsely populated Nordic areas (ERDF, ESF, EAGGF – Guidance section). In the 1999 reform, it was agreed that Objective 1 would continue to assist the least-developed regions, defined as those with a GDP per capita at 75% or less of the EU average over the previous three years. Henceforth, this criterion would be strictly enforced. In addition, the new Objective 1 included the regions that previously qualified under Objective 6, which were the sparsely populated regions of Finland and Sweden. Objectives 2 and 5b were merged into a new Objective 2, assisting 'areas undergoing socioeconomic change in the industrial and service sectors, and rural areas, urban areas and areas dependent on fisheries facing difficulties'. Objective 2 would be concentrated on no more than 18% of the EU population, with the safety-net mechanism ensuring that no member state's Objective 2 population would be less than two-thirds of its coverage under the 1994–1999 programme period. From 2000, Objective 3 would apply across the EU, except for in Objective 1 regions, and would assist in modernizing systems of education, training and employment.

7. The new *convergence* objective incorporated the old Objective 1 and the Cohesion Fund objectives (drawing on ERDF, ESF and Cohesion Fund); the new *regional competitiveness and employment objective* incorporated the old Objectives 2 and 3 (ERDF and ESF) and the new *European territorial cooperation objective* incorporated a number of Community Initiative programmes (ERDF).

References

Andreou, G. 2006. EU cohesion policy in Greece: Patterns of governance and Europeanization. *South European Society and Politics* 11, no. 4: 241–59.

Andreou, G. 2010. The domestic effects of EU cohesion policy in Greece: Islands of Europeanization in a sea of traditional practices. *Southeast European and Black Sea Studies* 10, no. 1: 13–27.

Bache, I. 2008. *Europeanization and multi-level governance: Cohesion policy in the European Union and Britain.* Lanham, MD/Oxford: Rowman and Littlefield.

Bache, I. 2010. Partnership as an EU policy instrument: A *political* history. *West European Politics* 33, no. 1: 58–74.

Bache, I., and A. Jordan. 2006. Europeanization and domestic change. In *The Europeanization of British politics*, ed. I. Bache and A. Jordan, 17–36. Basingstoke: Palgrave Macmillan.

Bachtler, J., and I. McMaster. 2008. EU cohesion policy and the role of the regions: Investigating the influence of structural funds in the new member states. *Environment and Planning C: Government and Policy* 26: 398–427.

Bailey, D., and L. De Propris. 2002. EU structural funds, regional capabilities and enlargement: Towards multi-level governance? *Journal of European Integration* 24: 303–24.

Börzel, T., and T. Risse. 2003. Conceptualising the domestic impact of Europe. In *The politics of Europeanization*, ed. K. Featherstone and C. Radaelli, 57–82. Oxford: Oxford University Press.

Bruszt, L. 2008. Multi-level governance – the eastern versions: Emerging patterns of developmental governance in the new member states. *Regional and Federal Studies* 18, no. 5: 607–27.

Bulmer, S. 2007. Theorizing Europeanization. In *Europeanization: New research agendas*, ed. P. Graziano and M. Vink, 46–58. Basingstoke: Palgrave Macmillan.

Bulmer, S., and M. Burch. 2006. Central government. In *The Europeanization of British politics*, ed. I. Bache and A. Jordan, 37–51. Basingstoke: Palgrave Macmillan.

Bulmer, S., and C. Radaelli. 2005. The Europeanisation of national policy. In *The member states of the European Union*, ed. S. Bulmer and C. Lesquesne, 338–59. Oxford: Oxford University Press.

DG Enlargement. 2007. *Financial instruments and EU enlargement projects.* http://ec.europa.eu/enlargement/financial_assistance/index_en.htm.

European Commission. 1993. *Community structural funds 1994–1999, revised regulations and comments.* Brussels/Luxembourg: European Communities.

Hooghe, L., ed. 1996. *Cohesion policy and European integration: Building multi-level governance.* Oxford: Oxford University Press.

Hughes, J., G. Sasse, and C. Gordon. 2004. Conditionality and compliance in the EU's eastward enlargement. *Journal of Common Market Studies* 42, no. 3: 523–51.

Hughes, J., G. Sasse, and C. Gordon. 2005. *Europeanization and regionalization in the EU's enlargement to Central and Eastern Europe: The myth of conditionality.* Basingstoke: Palgrave Macmillan.

Kohler-Koch, B. 1996. Catching up with change: The transformation of governance in the European Union. *Journal of European Public Policy* 3, no. 3: 359–80.

Leonardi, R. 2005. *Cohesion policy in the European Union: The building of Europe.* Basingstoke: Palgrave Macmillan.

March, J., and J. Olsen. 1998. *The institutional dynamics of international political orders.* Arena Working Papers WP 98/5. Oslo: Arena.

Marcou, G., ed. 2002. *Regionalization for development and accession to the European Union: A comparative perspective, local government and public service reform initiative.* Budapest: Open Society Institute.

Marks, G. 1993. Structural policy and multi-level governance in the EC. In *The state of the European Community. Vol. 2: The Maastricht debates and beyond*, ed. A. Cafruny and G. Rosenthal, 391–410. Boulder, CO: Lynne Rienner.

Marks, G., and L. Hooghe. 2004. Contrasting visions of multi-level governance. In *Multi-level governance*, ed. I. Bache and M. Flinders, 15–30. Oxford: Oxford University Press.

Olsen, J. 2002. The many faces of Europeanization. *Journal of Common Market Studies* 40: 921–52.

Paraskevopoulos, C. 2006. EU enlargement and multi-level governance in European policy-making: Actors, institutions and learning. In *Adapting to multi-level governance: Regional and environmental policies in cohesion and CEE countries*, ed C. Paraskevopoulos, P. Getemis, and N. Rees, 3–24. Aldershot: Ashgate.

Pierson, P. 2004. *Politics in time: History, institutions and social analysis.* Princeton, NJ/ Oxford: Princeton University Press.

Radaelli, C. 2003. The Europeanization of public policy. In *The politics of Europeanization*, ed. K. Featherstone and C. Radaelli, 27–56. Oxford: Oxford University Press.

Rhodes, R. 1988. *Beyond Westminster and Whitehall.* London: Unwin-Hyman.

Rhodes, R. 1997. *Understanding governance: Policy networks, reflexivity and accountability.* Buckingham: Open University Press.

Schimmelfennig, F., and U. Sedelmeier, eds. 2005. *The Europeanization of Central and Eastern Europe.* Ithaca, NY: Cornell University Press.

Schmidt, V. 2006. *Democracy in Europe.* Oxford: Oxford University Press.

Tavistock Institute. 1999. *The thematic evaluation of the partnership principle: Final synthesis report.* London: The Tavistock Evaluation and Development Review Unit.

Thielemann, E. 1999. Institutional change and European governance: An analysis of partnership. *Current Politics and Economics of Europe* 9, no. 3: 181–97.

Tilly, C. 1984. *Big structures, large processes, huge comparisons.* New York: Russell Sage Foundation.

The domestic effects of EU cohesion policy in Greece: islands of Europeanization in a sea of traditional practices

George Andreou

Department of Political Sciences, Aristotle University of Thessaloniki, Thessaloniki, Greece

This contribution considers whether European Union (EU) cohesion policy has contributed to the development of a more compound polity in Greece and, specifically, considers the extent to which there is a process of Europeanization characterized by emergent features of multi-level governance. After providing a brief background on the nature of domestic governance and politics, it reviews the development of cohesion policy instruments in Greece and, then, discusses the scope and the nature of changes that have taken place in the last decade. The main finding is that, while the effects of EU cohesion policy on Type I multi-level governance remain limited, its impact on Type II multi-level governance is more pronounced. However, change is neither omnipresent nor linear. The overall picture is one of an emerging archipelago of 'islands of Europeanization' within a sea of traditional institutions and practices.

Introduction

The goal of this study is to discuss the Europeanization effects of cohesion policy on governance in Greece. The second section provides a brief background on the nature of governance and politics in Greece. The third section gives an overview of the relevant European Union (EU) policy instruments operating in Greece, past and present. The fourth section includes the main findings from the interviews and other research undertaken for this article.[1] It highlights the main developments that have taken place in relation to multi-level governance before considering the vertical and horizontal dimensions, respectively (see Bache 2010). Section five examines the causes of domestic change and the 'Conclusion' argues that while the effects of EU cohesion policy on Type I multi-level governance remain limited, its impact on Type II multi-level governance[2] is more pronounced. However, change is neither omnipresent nor linear. The overall picture is one of a slightly more compound polity characterized by an emerging archipelago of 'islands of Europeanization' within a sea of traditional institutions and practices.

Governance and politics in Greece

Using Schmidt's (2006) typology on the nature of European democracies (see Bache 2010), Greece is a simple polity par excellence, combining a unitary state structure, a majoritarian system of representation and statist policy-making processes. Centralism, majoritarianism and statism are deeply embedded in Greek political tradition and culture; in fact, they are ever present in the historical pattern of development of modern Greece.

To begin with, the modern Greek state was built in the mould of the – centralized – French model of government. Moreover, the slow, piecemeal and disjointed process of Greece's national unification – lasting from the establishment of an independent Greek state in 1833 to the incorporation of the Dodecanese islands in 1948 – encouraged the strengthening of the central political and administrative institutions and, simultaneously, bred a widespread sense of aversion towards decentralization (Ioakimidis 1996, 343–4).

At the same time, Greek politics acquired a distinct flavour of 'clientelism', and the collusion between private interests and politicians led to the development of a spoils system. It has been argued that the Greek state not only shaped its economy and society but also supported the basic mechanisms for the incorporation of the masses into the political system by fostering and expanding clientelistic networks and by encouraging a populist mentality advanced by the political parties. As a result, Greek civil society lacked any autonomy towards the state, which managed to control any independent initiative coming from 'below'[3] (Lyrintzis 2002, 90).

Centralism and statism received a further boost after the Civil War (1946–1949), when the victors established an anti-communist regime that culminated in a seven-year long military dictatorship (1967–1974). The subsequent transition to liberal democracy and the accession to the European Community (1981) did not signify a radical break with the past. Clientelistic relations lost their personalized character, but resurfaced through the party structure and activity, thereby strengthening the parties' role and influence in policy.

State institutions, political parties and clientelism have pre-empted the space for independent activity by interest groups. However, while the labour unions remained dependent on the state (and the peak labour confederations suffered from internal factionalization along party lines), Greek business retained much of its organizational autonomy and developed considerable capabilities vis-à-vis political institutions (Lavdas 2005, 299–300).

Following Featherstone (2005, 228–30), the key features of Greek politics in the 1970s and 1980s were centralization, statism and over-regulation, conflictual inter-party relations, populism and clientelism, a weak civil service and, finally, a weak civil society and a problematic and 'disjointed' social dialogue. It is obvious that these characteristics stand in sharp contrast to the complex compound polity of the EU (Bache 2010).

In the last three decades – and especially since 1989 – Greece's 'exposure' to EU cohesion policy has generated strong pressures for domestic change towards a more compound direction through the promotion of multi-level governance. However, one should neither underestimate the resilience of domestic actors and institutions nor overestimate the transformative power of cohesion policy.[4] It would be then plausible to expect that (1) Greece's overall progress towards a compound polity would be rather limited, and (2) significant effects on Type I multi-level governance would be less likely than on Type II.

The main cohesion policies and instruments

The ERDF, the ESF and the Integrated Mediterranean Programmes (1981–1989)

The impact of the EU in the field of cohesion policy in Greece became evident even before EU membership (Verney 1994). However, 'governance effects' became visible only after the creation of the Integrated Mediterranean Programmes (IMPs) in 1985. The regulation for the IMPs stipulated that the Community would contribute 2 billion ECUs for Greece for the period 1985–1992.

More significantly, the IMPs introduced the new concepts of regionalization, programming and partnership. In response to these requirements, Greece was divided into six regions, although the division was purely administrative and limited institutionally to the monitoring committees required to oversee the IMPs. Then, 13 NUTS 2 administrative regions[5] (*peripheries*) were established in 1986; soon, these new entities were to take over the planning and management of cohesion policy at the regional level.

The Greek package of IMPs was drawn up at the central level (they were written by the regional policy department of the Ministry of National Economy, MNE) in a somewhat piecemeal manner, the fundamental concern of their authors being to achieve the maximum absorption of funds at the earliest possible time. The planning of the IMPs, then, appeared to become an exercise in centralized control and the stifling of local efforts (Papageorgiou and Verney 1992, 146–7). At the implementation stage, neither the ministries involved nor the new monitoring committees were given the essential means in terms of resources, expertise or information, to perform their tasks properly. In addition, the ultimate control over implementation was held by MNE (Ioakimidis 1996, 353–4). As a result, the IMPs have been often dismissed as a wasted opportunity. Yet they did signal the beginning of a process of decentralization and administrative adjustment, and, at the same time, they made the Commission more aware of the need to tighten up the conceptual framework of cohesion policy (Bianchi 1992, 68).

The first Community Support Framework (1989–1993)

The 1988 reform of the structural funds represented an even more serious challenge for the Greek politico-administrative system. Meeting the EU programming requirements was beyond the abilities of Greek government and administration (Ioannou 2001). The input of subnational actors was again limited, owing to the preponderance of sectoral development priorities and to the poor quality of the proposals submitted by the 13 regional secretaries after consultations with the prefectures (Ioakimidis 1996, 355). It would be thus more accurate to speak of a process of limited cooperation between the central government and its decentralized services rather than of a genuine partnership (DMP 1991, 87).

From 1989 to 1993, the overall financial envelope of cohesion policy in Greece reached 15.4 billion ECUs (in 1994 prices). The first Greek Community Support Framework (CSF) comprised 25 highly complex operational programmes (OPs) and was managed by the central government and administration. Besides, the promotion of regional development was but one objective of the first CSF – 40.9% of this was dedicated to this priority. Policy monitoring was undertaken by a monitoring committee for the CSF as a whole (under the MNE), assisted by the monitoring committees in charge of each of the 12 sectoral OPs and the 13 regional OPs. These monitoring committees were made up of national administrators (for the sectoral OPs) or regional and prefecture officials (for the regional OPs), Commission officials, a representative of MNE and representatives of the relevant social partners.

During the first CSF, implementation was left almost entirely to the devices of the pre-existing administrative system. The bulk of national efforts were targeted in increasing absorption rates, while the issue of implementation effectiveness was rarely addressed. In all, the experience of the first CSF suggested that very little was done to strengthen the participation of regional actors in the decision-making process and to promote a truly regional approach in policy-making (Andreou 2006; Verney 1994).

The second Community Support Framework (1994–1999)

During the second Greek CSF, EU's financial support was doubled in relation to the period 1989–1993. As a consequence, the EU co-financed programmes reached the amount of 34.76 billion ECUs (in 1994 prices). In all, there were 16 sectoral OPs and 13 regional OPs (EEO 2003, 107). The latter took a significantly lower share than in the first CSF (25.1% as opposed to 40.9%; EEO 2003, 5).

Throughout the negotiations on the adoption of the second CSF, the Commission pushed for the creation of structures as independent as possible from mainstream public administration, or at least structures endowed with transparent procedures and a high quality of human capital. This initiative bore fruit with the assent of MNE and despite considerable resistance from certain ministers, civil servants and implementation agencies.[6] Thus, although the official management and monitoring structures were not altered, the quality of policy-making was indeed improved – though implementation effectiveness varied greatly across individual OPs (Ioannou 2001, 258–69).

The most important aspect of partnership in Greece during the second CSF was the relationship between the Commission and the member state (Tavistock Institute 1999, 91). This process of interaction had a rather marginal impact on the performance of public (central and regional) administration. Moreover, the multiplication of communication channels between subnational and supranational actors and the mobilization of local interests contributed to the creation of various policy networks that, however, remained entangled in the national political game (Koutalakis 1997). Finally, although non-state actors' involvement in the policy process increased, it took mainly the form of recruitment within or under the guidance of specific ministries. On top of this, there was no evidence of extended private sector involvement in the regional OPs (Paraskevopoulos 2005, 460).

The third Community Support Framework (2000–2006)

The 1999 reforms in cohesion policy gave an extra impetus to the dynamics of 'technocratization' and 'de-politicization' favoured by both the Commission and the renamed Ministry of Economy and Finance (MEF) since 1994. In the course of the CSF negotiations, the Commission favoured a management system that would be immune from all outside interferences, while the Greek government wanted the new management bodies incorporated in the body of public administration. In the end, the Greek government's view prevailed: it was decided that each OP would be managed by a 'special service' falling under the authority of the responsible ministry or region. On the other hand, the Commission insisted on controlling and approving the installation of the new 'managing authorities', as well as the central management, paying and monitoring system and the new system of control (all of which were located at MEF).

Overall, the third CSF had a budget of €44.75 billion (2004 prices) and comprised 11 sectoral OPs and 13 regional OPs. The share of the latter remained virtually unchanged (25.8%, as opposed to 25.1% in the second CSF). In December 2000, the Greek government passed the legislation establishing the institutional framework in line with the principles laid down in the CSF.

The body in charge of overall management – the CSF managing authority – remained the same unit of MEF that had the same competence for the two previous CSFs (although it was upgraded in terms of personnel and infrastructure in order to carry out its many missions). Each OP was managed by a 'managing authority' belonging to the relevant ministry or region. All 'managing authorities' were organized in an identical manner, their personnel being either reposted civil servants or newly recruited. The supporting institutions set up in the preceding programming period were retained and placed in the service of the 'managing authorities'. Major steps were also made in relation to private sector involvement in the co-financing of CSF infrastructure projects.

The National Strategic Reference Framework and the new OPs (2007–2013)

For the 2007–2013 period, Greece has been allocated €20.42 billion in total (in 2006 prices). Once again, MEF was responsible for elaborating the National Strategic Reference Framework (NSRF) for 2007–2013 and for coordinating all the relevant procedures. In the words of MEF, 'the NSRF was elaborated in close cooperation with the relevant Ministries, Regional and Local Authorities and in deliberation with the EU, in the context of a more strengthened partnership compared to the previous period' (MEF 2006, 3). The programming period ended in November 2007, when the Commission approved the new OPs and the National Parliament adopted the law 'on the Management, Control and Implementation of Development Interventions for the Period 2007–2013' (Hellenic Republic 2007).

The programming architecture of 2007–2013 had to take into account the experience of the third CSF and, simultaneously, to respond to the realities of the new programming period.[7] MEF met these challenges by introducing two major changes (not without a certain amount of opposition by various line ministries):

- Firstly, the number of OPs has been reduced to 13 'domestic' OPs (eight sectoral OPs and five regional OPs) and 12 territorial cooperation OPs. Each of the new regional OPs (with the exception of Attica) covers three NUTS 2 regions.[8]
- Secondly, the five regions entering transitional support for the first time (Continental Greece, South Aegean, Attica, Central Macedonia and West Macedonia) were to receive 'differentiated treatment' (i.e. less generous funding and a more limited range of interventions) compared to the eight Objective 1 regions.

It is noteworthy that these programming changes were not accompanied by any significant *institutional* modifications; this point will be extensively discussed in the following section.

The nature and extent of domestic change

Key developments in the last decade

During the last 10 years, there has been a steady improvement regarding programming (European Commission DG Regio official, interview 2008). Moreover, there has been a broadening of participation since the second CSF [Development Company of West Macedonia (ANKO) official, interview 2008]. On the other hand, the situation has remained more or less the same in terms of the relative policy influence of the main actors.

Throughout the whole programming process (including the negotiations with the Commission), MEF plays a coordinating and gate-keeping role. The line ministries are involved in planning only when it comes to issues falling under their competence. On the other hand, the line ministries and, secondly, the regions are able to influence one single major component of the programming framework: the allocation of funding between the various OPs. Thus, the budget of each OP for the periods 2000–2006 and 2007–2013 was defined at the inter-ministerial level with the arbitration of the Prime Minister himself.

The essence of central programming is the creation of the overall programming architecture. MEF monopolizes this competence. Thus, 'broadening partner's responsibilities to all phases of programming' (MEF 2006, 3) means essentially that the main sectoral and regional actors were given the opportunities to 'fill in the details' within a well-defined and rigid framework. There are no permanent structures for sectoral and regional planning. Each ministry and region possesses a Directorate for Planning and Development, but these bodies lack the necessary resources to assume a strategic role. Unavoidably, then, this burden is transferred to the only institutions available: the 'managing authorities'.

As it has already been mentioned, one of the major changes in 2007–2013 has been the creation of four new regional OPs, each of which involved three regions. This restructuring has not been the result of a genuine strategy shift. Initially, the Greek government had attempted to reduce the number of Greek regions from 13 to 5 in order to maximize Objective 1 coverage for the country. However, the Commission refused to accept this change; as a result, Greek policy-makers were obliged to design five regional OPs for the 13 'old' regions.

The planners of the new regional OPs tried to legitimize the new approach by highlighting the common geographical and socio-economic features of the new planning entities and by undertaking a joint development analysis for each grouping. The Commission accepted this analysis purely for political reasons. Yet, the new planning logic does not extend to the programming content; each of the four new regional OPs is actually nothing more than the sum of three distinct development plans, each of which pertains to an 'old' region ('managing authority' of regional OP for Central Macedonia official, interview 2008).

The 2007–2013 implementation system is not radically different from the pre-existing one. Yet, contrary to the government's assertions, the changes introduced point towards more centralization (European Commission DG Regio official, interview 2008) and more complicated decision-making procedures, while there is also a greater diffusion of responsibility. To begin with, the division of labour between the sectoral and the regional OPs has changed. Under the new framework law (Hellenic Republic 2007), all regional OPs will be coordinated by a single 'managing authority' under MEF. This new body is going to delegate management competences to the 13 'old' regional 'managing authorities' (now renamed 'intermediate managing authorities') and to the sectoral 'managing authorities' covering European Regional Development Fund (ERDF) interventions.

Moreover, the range of interventions under the regional OPs has shrunk: in effect, they include mostly infrastructure projects under the ERDF. Besides, some line ministries are setting up new 'coordination authorities', their task being to coordinate the activities of the regional OPs in their policy field; henceforth, the regional 'intermediate managing authorities' will be obliged to acquire the consent of these coordinating bodies before approving the inclusion of concrete actions in the regional operational programmes. As a consequence, it is expected that the bureaucratic burden in decision-making will increase (managing authority of regional OP for Central Macedonia official, interview 2008). On the other hand, management responsibilities are devolved in 2007–2013. The establishment of new certification procedures will hopefully lead to the emergence of fewer and better endowed final beneficiaries; this development will improve the quality of management.[9]

The vertical dimension of multi-level governance

A key element of understanding the extent to which multi-level governance is emerging is to identify any shifts in power relations between key actors. The first thing to note on this here is that all interviewees recognized that the cohesion policy system in Greece is centralized and that MEF is the most important and most powerful actor. The importance of YPEHODE (the Ministry of the Environment and Public Works) and of the Ministry of Employment was also recognized by all. There was some disagreement between interviewees as to the importance of the Ministry of Development, which may stem from the difference in policy perspectives.[10] Other line ministries, such as the Ministry of Education and the Ministry of the Interior, were also mentioned as important, but on a less frequent basis.

Secondly, there was also a wide agreement among interviewees on the weakness of the Greek regions. This weakness is attributed to the inherent centralization bias of the Greek state and to the lack of resources of the regional administrations (Management Organization Unit official, interview 2008). The regions are much weaker than the ministries and are further weakened in the new programming period starting in 2007 because they no longer plan and administer individual OPs and also because their 'managing authorities' are placed officially under the leadership of the MEF. In addition, there is no social dialogue on strategy for the promotion of regional development and employment at the regional level. What is actually happening is that there is a state institution (the region) which arbitrates between subnational and social actors.

Given the above, it is no surprise that the implementation of the partnership principle in the framework of the monitoring committees is problematic. In the second CSF, the monitoring committees played a consultative role – the real decision-makers being the government and the European Commission. Under the third CSF, the monitoring committee has a decision-making role and all decisions are taken by simple majority. However, many participants do not possess the necessary economic, organizational and human resources to monitor systematically the implementation of the OPs. On top of that, government agencies do not provide systematic information regarding management and evaluation. Besides, the monitoring committees are convened very rarely (usually once a year or at even longer intervals).

Finally, in most instances, the OPs are amended by 'written procedure': the president of the monitoring committee sends a draft decision to all members, who are called to express their opinion within 20 days (or sooner, 'in very urgent cases'). The draft decision is deemed accepted after the simple majority of the voting members have expressed their consent; crucially, a lack of response within the prescribed deadline is considered as approval.[11] Finally, it is worth mentioning that the introduction of evaluation procedures has not led to greater accountability. There are relatively few quantitative targets and timetables which are often modified (manipulated) in line with programme amendments (General Confederation of Greek Workers official, interview 2008).

To conclude, local governments (prefectures and municipalities) are policy consumers rather than policy-makers. Although they lack the administrative, political, financial and informational resources to shape programmes significantly – usually favouring small-scale projects in the areas of infrastructure and training – they possess enough influence to place themselves in the list of final beneficiaries in a wide range of projects (mainly in the framework of the regional OPs). At the same time, they are vulnerable to clientelism and populism. As a result, they are often granted projects without having the necessary resources and capacity for management and monitoring (Management Organization Unit official, interview 2008).

At the same time, there has been a steady improvement in management quality since 1989. The first tuning point was the series of small-scale reforms introduced during the second CSF – the reform of the public works system, the creation of the first public–private partnerships and the establishment of the Management Organization Unit in 1996–1998 were the changes mentioned by most interviewees. However, the most important change was the foundation of a new management system in 2001–2003. The first beneficial effect of this change was that the system achieved some insulation from political interventions. Secondly, the level of professionalism has improved both at the level of the 'managing authorities' and at the level of the final beneficiaries.

That being said, it appears that power relations have not changed significantly, essentially because the overall policy framework has remained the same. This stability is reflected in the fact that, despite the change of the overall programming architecture for the period 2007–2013, all major actors (i.e. the most important ministries) retained their pre-existing roles, although in a modified guise. On the other hand, the newly instituted changes at the level of management hold the potential to enhance the autonomy of the final beneficiaries (many of which are subnational and social actors).

The horizontal dimension of multi-level governance

As noted in the introduction, civil society in Greece has traditionally been very weak. More specifically, the tradition of 'radial cooperation' with the state – each individual actor advances his own demands to the state and develops 'exclusive' ties with parts of the administration without interacting with other actors – encourages the development of 'patron–client relationships' and inhibits the articulation of collective interests and the elaboration of collective strategies. Besides, existent collective organizations are captured by political and/or particularistic interests. Social dialogue is very under-developed at the bottom (i.e. beyond the peak level), be it at the sectoral or at the regional level (General Confederation of Greek Workers official, interview 2008).

This deficit is manifest in the institutionalized participation of social partners in the monitoring committees of all the OPs – be they sectoral or regional – where only a fraction of the non-state participants are able to take part actively in the deliberations (Federation of Greek Industries official; General Confederation of Greek Workers official, interviews 2008). In general terms, the limited policy influence of social part-ners reflects their low degree of capability in the administrative, political, financial and informational realm (European Commission DG Regio official, interview 2008).

It appears that employer organizations are more active and influential than labour unions. This phenomenon could be attributed to the greater financial, institutional and organizational resources that business interests possess and also to the fact that direct support to business is a significant component of cohesion policy. Employer organizations are thus important players in the field of state aid (they have established development companies that have undertaken the management of portions of the OP 'Competitiveness').

Over time, an 'EU logic', placing emphasis on integrated planning and on consistent and rigorous management and monitoring, has been accepted by actors across the board. Having 'internalized' the principles of sound planning and management, the most important players (the ministries and the regions) have started speaking the same language (MEF Special Service for Strategy, Planning and Evaluation of Development Programmes official, interview 2008). The reforms of the late 1990s, the establishment of a new management system in 2001 and the growing planning and implementing maturity have certainly encouraged 'thick' learning through the promotion of partici-pation, meritocracy, transparency and accountability. However, the smaller subnational actors are inherently weak and often express a 'traditional' mentality, which can also be viewed as learning lag (Federation of Greek Industries official, interview 2008).

For instance, the ministries and the 'managing authorities' find it very difficult to convince the local authorities (prefectures and municipalities) to accept the distinction between 'hard' and 'soft' actions (MEF Special Service for Strategy, Planning and Evaluation of Development Programmes official, interview 2008). Some interviewees actually speak of 'resistance to change' in areas such as the environment and training. This attitude is understandable, taking into account that the older practice of granting projects according to political and party criteria, characterized as 'populism in plan-ning and implementation' ('managing authority' of regional OP for Central Mace-donia official, interview 2008), was not eliminated in the third CSF.

The role of experts has become more important with the passage of time. An illus-trative example of the growing importance of expertise is the 'managing authorities' themselves; their existence has led to a significant improvement in both the quantity and the quality of personnel (MEF Special Service for Strategy, Planning and Evalu-ation of Development Programmes official, interview 2008). The involvement of consultants reached its peak in the second CSF, when the lack of human resources was greater in the public administration. Since the creation of the 'managing authorities', the involvement of experts has been less extensive; however, the new managing bodies are still using outsourcing when their workload is too heavy (Federation of Industries of North Greece official, interview 2008).

That being so, one should not forget that expertise has increased mainly in the area of implementation, and that policy formulation remains a task of the conventional administration which remains untouched by reform. Therefore, there is still a great deficit in policy formulation and steering which inhibits efforts for the development of a common understanding and encourages approaches focusing on meeting the minimum EU requirements and safeguarding absorption (Management Organization Unit official, interview 2008).

Tracing the causes of domestic change

EU cohesion policy has had a significant impact on Greek structures, policies and politics. Yet, the EU influence did not manifest itself principally in the field of territorial relations, but in the domain of policy objectives, policy style and practices. Taking aside the creation of Greek regions (deemed necessary for the absorption of EU funds), this method did not involve institutional reform, but the 'patching up' of new policies and institutions onto existing ones – without changing the latter (Andreou 2006, 253).

A 'critical juncture' was triggered during the 1993–1999 funding period. At this particular moment, EU requirements and pressures, efficiency considerations and the bias towards centralization induced the pro-European and 'modernist' Simitis government to reform the management system, albeit in a form that did not undermine centralization. Thus, since 1996 Greece witnessed a multiplication of task-specific governing bodies which are operating at numerous territorial levels and are often overlapping (including 'managing authorities' at both the national and subnational level and various 'supporting bodies' operating at the national level). At the same time, many municipalities and prefectures have set up development companies, which, however, function mainly as policy consumers rather than policy-makers.

Under the 2000–2006 system, the allocation of competences between potential participants in implementation was not always clear; there were also some overlapping responsibilities. Various interviewees have also argued that the management procedures have been really complex. This complexity is not solely the outcome of the EU regulations: national legislation (the way the EU regulations are interpreted in the domestic context), instead of adjusting domestic rules and practices to EU requirements, has added a second layer of complexity (Management Organization Unit official, interview 2008). Policy performance is thus hampered, and the absence of clear rules is exploited by many actors who manipulate the rules in order to benefit from funding. In addition, the very 'heaviness' of the system creates many disincentives for the involvement of the private sector (European Commission DG Health official, interview 2008). Finally, despite the changes that have taken place in the last decade, policy delivery is still politicized and often 'micromanaged from the top' (European Commission DG Regio official, interview 2008).

The EU influence is strongest in the fields of management, evaluation and control. EU principles – integrated programming, partnership, transparency – and practices – sound management, evaluation and control – have been gradually incorporated into domestic practices. The obligations posed by the 1993 and 1999 regulations and Commission guidelines provided a strong incentive for the re-organization of the whole management system in a more rational and de-politicized way; this constituted a departure from the practices that were prevalent in 1985–1993.

Moreover, from the end of the first CSF, the Commission started promoting the idea of establishment of an independent management, evaluation and control system. These forces certainly had an impact on the content of the subsequent reforms that led to the radical reorganization of the Greek management system. The most striking example is the creation of the Management Organization Unit (the agency that took over the reorganization of the regional OPs in the second CSF and is now supporting the management of all OPs).

It is recognized that the CSFs and the NSRF, with all their shortcomings, have brought better governance. Day-to-day management according to EU standards has gradually led to the transfer and exchange of know-how. As a consequence, there is a spillover effect: the 'managing authorities' have become repositories of new skills and practices, which are gradually disseminated in the wider public sector. Yet only certain segments of the public administration are open to change – mostly the ministries and the bigger public enterprises.

Learning effects are still scarce at the subnational level – with a few exceptions such as the Development Company of West Macedonia (ANKO). On the other hand, policy content is shaped essentially by domestic actors. EU guidelines are certainly followed (e.g. regarding the coherence of the OPs with the Lisbon strategy and the setting of earmarking targets). However, these adjustments take place only at the level of principles and do not manifest themselves often at the level of actual policy-making. The most evident example of the persistence of domestic considerations is the endemic neglect of 'soft' actions such as training, R&D activities and measures promoting innovation and entrepreneurship.

Conclusion

As the discussion above has illustrated, EU cohesion policy has had a significant impact on the development of Type II multi-level governance in Greece and has thus nudged the Greek polity in a more compound direction. Since the second CSF, the central government has favoured the multiplication of task-specific governing bodies operating at numerous territorial levels. It can be argued that Europeanization pressures were 'accommodated' (Börzel and Risse 2000, 10) through 'layering'. On the one hand, the core of the pre-existing processes, policies and institutions remained unmodified. On the other hand, new layers of institutions were added in the system and were 'sold' as refinements of or correctives to the existing institutions (Streeck and Thelen 2005, 23). The establishment of special agencies outside the mainstream administration during the second CSF was feasible for two reasons. Firstly, the public sector was not amenable to any reform that would increase policy effectiveness *immediately*; such an initiative would produce significant adjustment costs and would have seriously challenged the political and administrative status quo. Secondly, the new layers did not directly undermine existing institutions and, thus, were tolerated by the mainstream public administration.

Developments in Type I multi-level governance are far less spectacular – and Greece remains one of the more centralized states of the EU. The only significant development was the establishment of the 13 administrative regions in 1989. However, the Greek regions were created in the mould of the traditional public administration; thus, they were the first public sector institutions that received an extra 'layer' (through the creation of special management bodies by the Management Organization Unit) at the end of the second CSF. Moreover, the new regional 'managing authorities' are not integrated in the regional administration and are not perceived as representatives of regional interests[12]; in effect, their creation has been interpreted as evidence of re-centralization (Getimis and Demetropoulou 2004, 356).

Top-down Europeanization effects are evident in the realm of management and implementation. The managing network created in 2001 operates on a different logic to the system that was set up in 1989, and which could not meet the principles and standards of cohesion policy, focusing instead on maximizing absorption: greater emphasis is placed on transparency, accountability and policy effectiveness. These changes were dictated both by strategic calculations and, progressively, by (thick) learning. In the first place, Greece had to comply with the new regulations and show some responsiveness to Commission criticisms; otherwise the inflow of EU funds would have been jeopardized. On the other hand, the manifest policy failure of the first CSF and the accumulation of experience militated for reform and for some degree of adjustment to EU norms.

Once the new institutions were established, a dynamic of deep learning became evident and policy performance was gradually increased. In this respect, the EU was certainly the catalyst for change. At the same time, the state encouraged the establishment of more specialized institutions under different guises (mostly *Societes Anonymes* controlled by the ministries, the regions and/or the local governments). Yet the performance of these entities is very uneven; in general, local development companies are underperforming because they are the fruit of 'thin learning' (ANKO official, interview 2008).

'Thick learning' is more manifest at the central level ('managing authority' of the Cohesion Fund official, interview 2008), in the peak employer organizations (Federation of Greek Industries official, interview 2008) and in the technical professions (Egnatia Odos S.A. official, interview 2008). This development is reflected in increases in policy effectiveness, in the adoption and diffusion of new management techniques and in the dissemination – and even the export – of good practices. The introduction of a more demanding system for the certification of all final beneficiaries is an additional step forward in this respect.

To conclude, cohesion policy has generated an asymmetrical and uncertain process of change in Greece. The establishment of a semi-autonomous 'parallel administration' in the third CSF generated processes of 'thick learning', leading to the proliferation of new practices and policy improvements. Although these developments did not have an immediate effect on the role and performance of the mainstream administration beyond the public works system, there are indications that more policy fields are being Europeanized in the last decade (e.g. public investment, environmental policy). At the risk of oversimplification, it can thus be argued that the overall picture in Greece is one of an emerging archipelago of 'islands of Europeanization' within a sea of traditional institutions and practices.

Acknowledgements

This study draws on research funded by the UK Economic and Social Research Council (Multi-level Governance in Southeast Europe, ESRC grant no. RES-062-23-0183). I would like to thank the ESRC for its support and my co-editor Ian Bache and the two anonymous referees for the journal for their helpful comments on earlier versions of this article. All the usual disclaimers apply.

Notes

1. Between 11 January 2008 and 11 September 2008, 12 semi-structured interviews were conducted with representatives of the following organizations: Ministry of Economy and

Finance (MEF), central 'managing authority' of CSF and Cohesion Fund: (i) Special Service for Strategy, Planning and Evaluation of Development Programmes, and (ii) 'managing authority' of the Cohesion Fund; Federation of Greek Industries (SEV); Ministry of Development, 'managing authority' of the OP 'Competitiveness'; General Confederation of Greek Workers (INE-GSEE); Management Organization Unit S.A.; 'managing authority' of the regional operational programme Central Macedonia; Development Agency of West Macedonia S.A. (ANKO); Federation of Industries of North Greece (SVVE); Egnatia Odos S.A.; the European Commission Directorate for Regional Policy; the European Commission Directorate for Health.
2. Here we draw on the two types of multi-level governance developed by Marks and Hooghe (2004; see also Bache 2010). Type I multi-level governance describes system-wide governing arrangements in which the dispersion of authority is restricted to a limited number of clearly defined, non-overlapping jurisdictions at a limited number of territorial levels, each of which has responsibility for a 'bundle' of functions. By contrast, Type II multi-level governance describes governing arrangements in which the jurisdiction of authority is task-specific, where jurisdictions operate at numerous territorial levels and may be overlapping.
3. The emergence of pluralistic structures was also undermined by 'objective factors' such as limited industrialization, weak class structures, disorientation from the influx of refugees and rapid urbanization (Featherstone and Yannopoulos 1995, 252).
4. The conceptual ambiguity and shifting priorities of cohesion policy, and the principles it represents, the lack of mechanisms of legal enforcement and the sequential nature of the related decision-making processes provide ample opportunity structures to domestic actors and institutions (Andreou 2006, 243).
5. For an explanation of the NUTS classification system, see Bache (2010).
6. The institutions that were finally established were the Management Organization Unit S.A. (MOD) – a semi-independent body operating under private law responsible for the supply of advice, administrative tools and know-how to the monitoring authorities and the implementation agencies-, a specialized agency for the attraction of private investment (ELKE), the Joint Steering Committee for Public Works (MEK), the Expert Agent for the Sampled Quality Control of Infrastructure Projects (ESPEL) and the National Accreditation Centre for Continuing Vocational Training (EKEPIS). Moreover, a number of semi-independent companies were set up in for the management of big infrastructure projects according to the Public–Private Partnership model.
7. Five Greek regions, containing 63% of the country's population, entered in a state of transitional support. Moreover, the new regulations provided for the establishment of a more decentralized system (whereby management responsibilities are transferred from the level of the CSF to the level of the OPs). On top of that, each of the new OPs had to be financed by either ERDF (with the possible support of the Cohesion Fund) or by the European Social Fund (ESF).
8. The five new regional OPs are the following: (i) regional OP 'Macedonia – Thrace' (covering the regions of Central Macedonia, West Macedonia and Eastern Macedonia – Thrace), (ii) regional OP 'West Greece – Peloponnesus – Ionian Islands', (iii) regional OP 'Crete and Aegean Islands' (covering the regions of Crete, North Aegean and South Aegean), (iv) regional OP 'Thessaly – Continental Greece – Eprius', and (v) regional OP 'Attica'.
9. There is a new government plan for the enhancement of the capacity of final beneficiaries until 2009. The main objective is to allocate projects and funds according to merit and not according to political criteria (interview, 'managing authority' of regional OP 'Central Macedonia' official, 2008; ANKO official, 2008).
10. For instance, two officials from the Federation of Greek Industrialists and the Federation of Industries of Northern Greece (two institutions that interact very often with the Ministry of Development) regarded it as the third most important institution. Conversely, an official from the 'managing authority' for the Cohesion Fund (that oversees the construction of big infrastructure projects in the areas of transport and environment) thought that the Ministry of Development was not very influential and instead placed the Ministry of Transport in the third position (a view that was not shared by any other interviewee).
11. As deadlines are tight, most monitoring committee members do not even have the time (let alone the resources) to form a view on the issues in question.

12. They have a specific legal status; they are task-specific; they are staffed by technocrats selected by a central institution; they operate according to 'Europeanized' rules and are accountable to the MEF.

References

Andreou, G. 2006. EU cohesion policy in Greece: Patterns of governance and Europeanization. *South European Society and Politics* 11, no. 2: 241–59.

Bache, I. 2010. Europeanization and multi-level governance: EU cohesion policy and pre-accession aid in Southeast Europe. *Southeast European and Black Sea Studies* 10, no. 1: 1–12.

Bianchi, G. 1992. The IMPs: A missed opportunity? *Regional Politics and Policy* 2, nos. 1–2: 47–70.

Börzel, T., and T. Risse. 2000. When Europe hits home: Europeanization and domestic change. *European Integration Online Papers* 4, no. 15. http://eiop.or.at/eiop/texte/2000-015a.htm.

DMP (Development Monitoring and Planning Ltd.). 1991. Evaluation report of the Community Support Framework for Greece [in French]. Athens.

EEO (European Enterprise Organisation S.A.). 2003. *Ex-post evaluation of the Objective 1, 1994–1999.* National Report, Athens.

Featherstone, K. 2005. Introduction: 'Modernisation' and the structural constraints of Greek politics. *West European Politics* 28, no. 2: 223–41.

Featherstone, K., and G. Yannopoulos. 1995. The European community and Greece: Integration and the challenge to centralism. In *The European Union and the regions*, ed. B. Jones and M. Keating, 249–66. Oxford: Clarendon Press.

Getimis, P., and L. Demetropoulou. 2004. Towards new forms of regional governance in Greece: The Southern Aegean Islands. *Regional and Federal Studies* 14, no. 3: 355–78.

Hellenic Republic. 2007. Law 3614/2007: On the management, control and implementation of development interventions for the period 2007–2013 [in Greek]. OJ 267/A, December 3, 2007.

Ioakimidis, P.C. 1996. EU cohesion policy in Greece: The tension between bureaucratic centralism and regionalism. In *Cohesion policy and European integration: Building multi-level governance*, ed. L. Hooghe, 342–66. Oxford: Oxford University Press.

Ioannou, D. 2001. Institutions, development and European regional policy in Greece, 1981–1999. PhD diss., Centre of International Studies, Faculty of History, University of Cambridge.

Koutalakis, C. 1997. Local development strategies in the EU: An evaluation of their impact on the Greek system of local governance. Paper presented at the final workshops on the European Policy Process organized by the Human Capital and Mobility Network, May 8–10, in Dublin.

Lavdas, K. 2005. Interest groups in disjointed corporatism: Social dialogue in Greece and European 'competitive corporatism'. *West European Politics* 28, no. 2: 297–316.

Lyrintzis, C. 2002. Greek civil society in the 21st century. In *Greece in the European Union: The new role and the new agenda*, ed. P.C. Ioakimidis, 90–9. Athens: Ministry of the Press and Mass Media.

Marks, G., and L. Hooghe. 2004. Contrasting visions of multi-level governance. In *Multi-level governance*, ed. I. Bache and M. Flinders, 15–30. Oxford: Oxford University Press.

MEF (Ministry of Economy and Finance). 2006. National Strategic Reference Framework, 2007–2013. October. Athens.

Papageorgiou, F., and S. Verney. 1992. Regional planning and the integrated mediterranean programmes in Greece. *Regional Politics and Policy* 2, nos. 1–2: 139–61.

Paraskevopoulos, C. 2005. Developing infrastructure as a learning process in Greece. *West European Politics* 28, no. 2: 445–70.

Schmidt, V. 2006. *Democracy in Europe.* Oxford: Oxford University Press.

Streeck, W., and K. Thelen, eds. 2005. Introduction: Institutional change in advanced political economies. In *Beyond continuity: Institutional change in advanced political economies*, 2–39. Oxford: Oxford University Press.

Tavistock Institute. 1999. *The thematic evaluation of the partnership principle: Final synthesis report.* http://www.europa.eu.int/regional_policy/sources/docgener/evaluation/rathe_en.htm.

Verney, S. 1994. Central state–local government relations. In *Greece and EU membership evaluated*, ed. P. Kazakos and P.C. Ioakimidis, 166–80. London: Pinter.

Europeanization and multi-level governance in Slovenia

George Andreou[a] and Ian Bache[b]

[a]Department of Political Sciences, Aristotle University of Thessaloniki, Thessaloniki, Greece;
[b]Department of Politics, University of Sheffield, Sheffield, UK

This study considers whether EU cohesion policy has contributed to the development of a more compound polity in Slovenia and, specifically, considers the extent to which there is a process of Europeanization characterized by emergent features of multi-level governance. After providing a brief background on the nature of domestic governance and politics, it reviews the development of cohesion policy instruments in Slovenia and, then, discusses the scope and the nature of changes that have taken place in the last decade. The main finding is that despite the pre-existing corporatist tradition suggesting a greater openness to cross-sectoral engagement than in most new member states, this tradition has little impact on the domestic approach to governing the structural funds. Only a weak system of multi-level governance has been developed, meeting the letter rather than the spirit of EU requirements, with central government ministries dominating both planning and implementation processes.

Introduction

This study considers whether EU cohesion policy has contributed to the development of a more compound polity in Slovenia and, specifically, considers the extent to which there is a process of Europeanization characterized by emergent features of multi-level governance. The next section provides a brief background on the nature of governance and politics in Slovenia. The third gives an overview of the relevant EU policy instruments operating in Slovenia, past and present. The fourth and fifth sections include the main findings from the interviews and other research undertaken.[1] They highlight the main developments that have taken place in relation to multi-level governance before considering the vertical and horizontal dimensions, respectively. The last section reflects on the main findings and considers their significance for the Slovenian polity.

Slovenia does not fit easily into the distinction between simple and compound polities (see Bache 2010), as it combines a unitary state structure, a proportional system of representation and corporatist policy-making processes. Slovenia's corporatist culture can be traced back to the Yugoslav period, while centralism and proportional representation were formulated and consolidated during the 'triple transition'[2] that took place after 1991, when the country gained its independence.

While centralism remains prominent, Slovenia is the most compound of the polities covered in this volume. It is also the smallest state covered with a land mass of 20,273 km² and a population of approximately two million. From this brief description, we might assume that the degree of fit with EU cohesion policy requirements on the horizontal dimension of multi-level governance (cross-sectoral engagement) would be relatively high, but on the vertical dimension (multi-level engagement) would be relatively low. Our purpose here is to explore whether this assumption holds true.

Governance and politics in Slovenia

Following the dissolution of the Austro-Hungarian monarchy in 1918, the territory of what is today Slovenia was split between Italy and Yugoslavia and shared the political and economic developments of these two countries. After the Second World War, the present territory of Slovenia became a constituent part of the Socialist Federal Republic of Yugoslavia. The latter was gradually transformed from a highly centralized socialist state in the 1950s and 1960s to a 'more efficient socialist system closer to the people' (Kovac 2007, 96) – which delegated a considerable amount of authority to local self-managed communities – in the 1970s.

Although official claims about the development of a grassroots-level self-government were exaggerated, these reforms did give ordinary people a limited but real input in decision-making at the workplace. Elements of pluralism also existed in numerous professional and occupational bodies, in the academy of science, and around some literary and social science journals, not to mention religious communities, clubs, study groups and other bodies affiliated with churches, and especially the Roman Catholic Church (Bebler 2002, 130).

The self-management system lasted for no more than 15 years. In the late 1980s, though still a Yugoslav republic, Slovenia introduced a multi-party system and, at the start of the 1990s, declared independence and undertook the transformation to private ownership and a market-based economy. The institutions of the self-management system were dismantled and in a very short time replaced by governmental services and a centralized tax system. The privatization of previously socially owned companies was put in hand, with the result that the erstwhile rather highly developed feeling of corporate social responsibility, with companies deeply involved in local, social and cultural development, was rapidly dissipated.

Pronounced to be a socialist illusion, social ownership was transformed by the new law on privatization into state or private ownership (Kovac 2007, 96–8). On the other hand, Slovenia chose a gradual path to the market. Changes were implemented on a step-by-step basis and liberalization coexisted with efforts to shield the economy from dramatic shocks. On top of that, relatively generous social welfare provisions, public works programmes and unemployment protection helped to protect workers from the adverse effects of market competition (Feldmann 2007, 330).

Since 1991, Slovenia has seen a high degree of centralization in resources and decision-making. Nowadays, Slovenia is a unitary state with two tiers of administration – the central government and 210 municipalities. The latter deal with issues of local importance and matters allocated to them by statute. There are also 58 administrative units, established in the 1993 reform of local self-government, performing public administration tasks with a territorial dimension. As a rule, these units cover one or more municipalities.

In addition, under pressure from the EU, 12 NUTS 3 development regions[3] were established by the first Law on Balanced Regional Development in 1999. In this context, regional development authorities (RDAs) with decision-making powers were introduced to promote regional development, based on the association of municipalities. Their role is limited to statistical purposes and to the planning of EU cohesion policy at the sub-national level, including participation in the preparation of regional development programmes (European Policies Research Centre 2008, 1).

As the establishment of entirely new institutional state structures and macroeconomic challenges of transitions dominated the political agenda in the first half of the 1990s, issues of sub-national governance reform were sidelined. Given that the Slovenian municipalities have limited political power, financial resources and administrative capacity – and have been more competitive than cohesive in their political aims – municipalities have not posed much of a challenge 'from below' to centralized political power. On top of that, societal actors and social partners have also organized their activities at the national, rather than regional, level (Lindstrom 2005, 4–5). However, since the beginning of the 2000s, a key debate has been underway on filling the gap between the central government and the municipalities, as well as on the number and functions of any new territorial entities (Faro 2004; Lajh 2004).

A constitutional amendment in June 2006 introduced *provinces* as a new level of government. Their remit includes: economic, social and cultural development; spatial development and environmental protection; traffic and transport links within the province; and providing public utilities of provincial significance. Based on the constitutional amendment, a province legislation package, consisting of five laws, was prepared by the government and discussed in the Parliament. The most important element of the package concerned the area definition, names and administrative seats of 14 proposed provinces. The passage of the law required a two-thirds majority. However, the province legislation package did not pass the Parliament in February 2008; a consultative referendum was held on the issue in June 2008, but the legitimacy of the referendum was questioned due to poor turnout.

Parliamentarism, corporatism and proportional representation are dominant features of political life in Slovenia. The bicameral Slovenian Parliament is composed of the National Assembly and the National Council. The specific social structure and historical development of Slovenia have prompted the creation of a bicameral system comprising the representation of political parties in the National Assembly and the representation of organized social interests and local authorities in the State Council. The Slovenian Parliament is characterized by an asymmetric duality, as the Constitution does not accord equal powers to both chambers. On the one hand, the National Assembly is Slovenia's central political institution. On the other hand, the National Council, despite its purely advisory role, is deemed to counterbalance the party representation in the National Assembly (Buchen 2005, 10). The principle of corporate representation is further enhanced by the existence of a tripartite Social-Economic Council (representing trade unions, employers and the government), which has served as facilitator of compromise solutions (Bebler 2002, 136–7) and which has been exerting a growing influence on setting standards with respect to economic and social policies (Buchen 2005, 10).

The deputies of the National Assembly (with the exception of two representatives of the Hungarian and Italian ethnic community, respectively) are elected by proportional representation, with a 4% threshold required at the national level. As a consequence, no single party has ever been strong enough to form a government on its own. Coalitions among the various parliamentary parties (which have varied in number from six to eight over the last decade) have become a way of life. Despite their occasional awkwardness and instability, these coalitions have become a major tool for crafting consensus (Bebler 2002, 133).

Slovenia can be seen as a coordinated market economy (Feldmann 2007). Industrial relations are dominated by a corporatist culture reflected in strong employers' associations and unions with far-reaching wage agreements. Wage-bargaining agreements cover a large portion of workers, who have considerable power through co-determination legislation, including work councils.[4] The most influential employers' organization is the Slovenian Chamber of Commerce and Industry. There are six umbrella employee associations; the dominant one is the Association of Free Trade Unions (an organization originating in communist times), which represents about half of the organized workforce. Employment protection and unemployment protection are very generous. Furthermore, there is a stakeholder approach to corporate governance, with a two-tier board structure securing representation of both workers and others.

Cohesion policy and pre-accession instruments

There are three distinct periods in Slovenia's participation in EU cohesion policy and relevant pre-accession instruments: pre-accession (1998–2004), post-accession (2004–2006) and the new financial perspective (2007–2013). Slovenia became eligible for pre-accession aid in 1998, getting the opportunity to obtain Phare and ISPA funds. The Phare funds were mainly aimed at strengthening environmental protection, regional development and especially at strengthening cross-border cooperation with neighbouring EU countries: Austria and Italy. The ISPA funds were mainly aimed at building environmental infrastructure (waste water systems, water supply systems, waste management, etc.), while twinning projects helped Slovenian government to adopt its legislation to EU standards. After becoming a full EU member, Slovenia became eligible for Objective 1 of the structural funding and for the Cohesion Fund. For the 2007–2013 period, all of Slovenia is eligible under the new convergence objective and has been allocated €4.101 billion (current prices) of funding. To complement the EU investment, Slovenia's overall annual contribution is expected to reach €957 million.

The institutional setting 1999–2008

The Slovenian system of cohesion policy management and implementation is complex and has undergone multiple changes over the last 10 years.[5] The general approach is framed by two important legal acts adopted in 1999: the Law on Balanced Regional Development, establishing a basic institutional framework for the implementation of the *acquis communautaire* under the chapter 'Regional Policy and Coordination of Structural Instruments'; and the Public Finance Act. Until 2000, responsibility for regional policy lay within the Ministry of Economic Relations and Development. After national elections in 2000, however, responsibility was transferred to the Ministry of Economy.

Between 2000 and 2002, planning and management competences were divided between the Ministry of Economy, being in charge of policy design, the Council for Structural Policy (set up in 2000 by the government), being responsible for coordinating proposals for structural policy implementation at the national level, and for designing and coordinating national development incentives and EU assistance, and the National Agency for Regional Development (NARD), which had important responsibilities for the daily management and coordination of national and EU regional policies.

In December 2002, the tasks of policy design and coordination were transferred to the newly created Government Office for Structural Policies and Regional Development (GOSP), headed by a minister without portfolio. In the period between 2003 and 2005, GOSP had to cooperate closely with NARD. The latter's aim was to coordinate, promote and implement a policy for balanced and sustainable regional development, while the former provided overall guidance and monitored the implementation of the NARD work programme and the 'Public Fund for Regional Development and the Preservation of the Settlement of Rural Areas'. Meanwhile, the role of the Council for Structural Policy decreased (with its last meeting taking place in 2003) and its functions were taken over by new forms of coordination, such as the Council for Sustainable Development, weekly meetings of ministers involved in structural funds implementation and Programme Councils.

After a change of government in 2004, the institutional apparatus for the management of cohesion policy underwent a new series of modifications. In 2005, the Government Office for Local Self-Government and Regional Policy (GORP) was set up after the merger of GOSP and the Directorate for Local Self-Government located in the Ministry of the Interior. With the adoption of a new Law on Balanced Regional Development in 2005, NARD became a part of GORP and was effectively abolished in January 2006. Since then, GORP has become the central coordinator of policy, although much of the policy input comes from other ministries that have policy responsibilities in their respective fields. GORP remains responsible for overall policy coordination and for direct negotiations with the European Commission and was involved in the whole process of preparation and implementation of cohesion policy on all levels (European, national and regional). In the current programming period, it is the sole managing authority of all three national operational programmes[6] (on Strengthening Regional Development Potentials, on Environmental and Transport Infrastructure Development and on Human Resources Development).

At the sub-national level, the 1999 Promotion of Balanced Regional Development Act laid out the conditions for forming RDAs. Conforming to the 12 new NUTS 3 regions, 12 new RDAs were established in 2001, tasked with implementing structural and cohesion programmes.[7] They are overseen by regional councils consisting of municipal mayors. The RDAs are responsible for coordinating, implementing and monitoring regional development programmes. Between 2002 and 2004, each RDA completed their respective development programmes, in coordination with NARD, for the programming period of 2002–2006. Some of the programmes were taken into account in the preparation of the National Development Plan (prepared in December 2001) which represented a strategic basis for Slovenia's preparation for its participation in cohesion policy as an EU member. However, the RDAs' performance in this instance was characterized as 'lacklustre at best, albeit with some RDAs outperforming others' (Lindstrom 2005, 11).

Key developments

1998–2004

During the pre-accession period, the pattern of the preparation and implementation of the EU's assistance programmes in Slovenia was as follows. The scope and overall level of funds from pre-accession assistance was agreed with the European Commission every year. Then, Slovenia first submitted several strategic documents (i.e. the *2000–2002 Preliminary Development Plan for Phare*, the *2000–2006 ISPA Strategy of Environmental and Transport Investments*, the Sapard-related *Seven-year Rural Development Plan* and the *National Development Plan for 2001–2006*, which encompassed the three strategic documents).

Following the submission of these strategic documents, within the so-called Phare Managing Committee, all details were harmonized and the Financial Memorandum signed. In this memorandum, the Commission agreed an ensured amount of funding. Accordingly, individual projects were implemented at the national and the sub-national level – either directly from a particular sectoral ministry or by other (implementing) agencies at the national, regional or local levels. Implementation of the programmes was accompanied by monitoring, evaluation and control processes (Lajh 2004, 20–1).

The major administrative issue in this period related to the territorial basis on which funds would be implemented post-accession. The controversy surrounding the creation of NUTS 2 regions in Slovenia involved heated discussions and negotiations on two levels: on the European level (i.e. between the EU and the Slovenian national government) and on the domestic level (i.e. between the national government and local municipalities). In the course of the pre-accession negotiations on the regional policy chapter, both Slovenia and the Commission fully reversed their earlier positions on the question of Slovenia's regionalization. Thus, in the final months of the negotiations, Slovenia requested that it should be allowed three regions (Eastern, Western and Capital) for the purpose of structural fund allocations, while the Commission's perspective was that Slovenia is too small to warrant more than a single region[8] (Faro 2004, 4).

At the domestic level the regionalization debate was overshadowed by the objections of the municipalities to both the government's three-region plan and the Commission's one-region proposal. Municipalities' objections were threefold. First, they cited statistics showing significant regional disparities in economic development. Second, they objected to the Commission's proposal by pointing out that this would lead to the concentration of power in Ljubljana, with the central government effectively controlling regional development planning and funding, as NUTS 3 regions cannot apply for project financing from the structural funds directly. Finally, they argued that if Slovenia remained a single NUTS 2 region this would undermine the ability of individual regions to lobby directly at the EU level to pursue their regional interests.

Accession negotiations were closed without the issue resolved, with both the Slovenian government and the Commission agreeing to postpone a final decision until 2006 (Lindstrom 2005, 8–9).

2004–2006

In line with the EU programming requirements, Slovenia had to prepare a *Single Programming Document* (SPD) for the period 2004–2006. The basic strategic documents, providing directions for the use of structural funds in the period 2004–2006, were the *Strategy of Economic Development of the Republic of Slovenia 2001–2006* and the *National Development Programme 2001–2006*. These laid the background for the SPD itself, which was drafted during the pre-accession period by GOSP in accordance with EU guidance.

Coordination with partners in this process took place on two levels. On the one hand, GOSP instructed the relevant line ministries (the Ministry of Labour, Family and Social Affairs as fund-related ministry for the European Social Fund (ESF), the Ministry of Agriculture, Forestry and Food as fund-related ministry for the European Agricultural Guarantee and Guidance Fund (EAGGF – Guidance), the Ministry of Economy as fund-related ministry for the European Regional Development Fund (ERDF)) to cooperate with partners when forming their proposals. This dimension was especially stressed when discussing horizontal, cross-cutting issues.

The document explains how the activities developed by the Ministry of Labour, Family and Social Affairs were 'systematically presented and discussed in a range of meetings, seminars and workshops' (GOSP 2003, 18); the Ministry of Agriculture, Forestry and Food 'set up various working groups composed of other line ministries' representatives, experts, NGOs and potential final beneficiaries'; and the Ministry of Economy was the first ministry to establish a 'programme council', which was an inter-ministerial institution involving state secretaries before organizing workshops and other activities for consultation. For ERDF, there was a specific engagement between the Ministry of Environment, Spatial Planning and Energy and environmental NGOs which wanted a stronger and more explicit environmental dimension in the SPD and that explicit environmental criteria be developed for project selection.

At the level of the overall SPD, a 'presentations and consultations process', directed to social partners, professional and economic associations, NGOs, local authorities, regional development agencies and the wider public, was led by GOSP itself (GOSP 2003, 18–20). This included consultations in all Slovene (NUTS 3) regions between March and April 2003. There was also a NDP/SPD monitoring committee, through which views were sought.

The draft SPD was forwarded to the European Commission in December 2003. Negotiations between the Commission and the Slovenian government followed, and the SPD was officially approved in June 2004. There was a single sectoral Objective 1 programme, co-financed by ERDF, ESF, EAGGF and FIFG (Financial Instrument for Fisheries Guidance), that reached the amount of €337 million (in 2004 prices), the EU contribution being €237.5 million. Moreover, €188.7 million was earmarked for Slovenia from the Cohesion Fund. The Objective 1 programme had three main objectives: (1) promotion of the productive sector and competitiveness; (2) knowledge, human resource development and employment; and (3) restructuring of agriculture, forestry and fisheries.

On the basis of the experience acquired during the implementation of pre-accession instruments, it was decided to maintain centralized institutional arrangements for the management of structural and cohesion funds. There was one managing authority (GORP) and one paying authority (the Ministry of Finance). In their role as Intermediate Bodies, three ministries – the Ministry of Economy (ERDF), the Ministry of Labour, Family and Social Affairs (ESF) and the Ministry of Agriculture, Forestry and Food (EAGGF and FIFG) – were responsible for the coordination of activities supporting individual Funds.

The managing authority was responsible for the overall coordination of programme preparation, including negotiations with the European Commission and with the three fund-related ministries. From March 2006, only the Ministry of Agriculture, Forestry and Food remained as an Intermediate Body. The transfer of Intermediate Body functions for ESF and ERDF to the managing authority eliminated one level of coordination and aimed to significantly improve the responsiveness, effectiveness and transparency of the system.

Overall, the 2004–2006 period was characterized by an approach based on learning-by-doing, reflected in multiple institutional changes. The fact that, notably at the beginning, too many organizations were involved meant that the system was not transparent, and decision-making responsibilities were not always clear. High levels of staff turnover contributed to this situation. Implementation problems were also caused by the relatively late start made to implementation and inadequate preparation of the administrative bodies (with too much reliance placed on the positive experiences under pre-accession assistance). The slow start led to much criticism and made the issue a political priority for the new government elected in 2004. As compared to existing domestic structures, the system for structural funds management was new in many respects. In a context characterized by a general lack of communication, the main innovation was that the system entailed improved inter-ministerial coordination and sustained efforts to achieve synergies among involved actors (European Policies Research Centre 2008, 13–14).

The new financial perspective: 2007–2013

In November 2005, during the peak of EU negotiations on the financial perspective, the Slovenian government introduced two NUTS 2 statistical regions: Eastern Slovenia and Western Slovenia[9] (GORP 2007, 15). The establishment of these new 'cohesion regions'[10] did not pertain on the eligibility rules for Slovenia for the 2007–2013 period (the structural funds regulations are still treating Slovenia as one NUTS 2 region) and thus had no immediate impact on the level and the distribution of EU funding for the country. However, the existence of the new regional entities would surely affect cohesion funding *after* 2013, when less affluent Eastern Slovenia would be entitled to a higher level of assistance than the one it would receive as a part of a country-wide NUTS 2 region. The introduction of two NUTS 2 regions must then be viewed as a strategic move aiming at maximizing EU funding for Slovenia in the long run.

In compliance with the structural fund regulations, Slovenia had to prepare a National Strategic Reference Framework (NSRF), defining its national strategy for achieving faster convergence, particularly through the contribution of the EU funds, and a number of operational programmes, each specifying the nature and the goals of co-financed interventions in a certain policy domain. The whole exercise was coordinated by GORP, which initiated a series of public presentations and consultations with a number of domestic stakeholders (including regional and local bodies), as well as with the European Commission.

Then, a special inter-ministerial group was formed and a number of key government bodies were selected to participate in the preparation of the NSRF by submitting official proposals.[11] A draft NSRF was produced in September 2006, and a number of consultations with NGOs, social partners and regional and local bodies followed (GORP 2007, 6–13). In parallel, Slovenia prepared a National Development Plan and 12 regional development plans for each NUTS 3 statistical region. The regional development plans consist of two parts: the strategic and the implementation part, with the latter containing project proposals for spending cohesion funds.

On 16 February 2007, GORP finalized the official proposal of the programming documents (the NSRF and three operational programmes described above) and forwarded them to the European Commission. Finally, after informal consultations between the government and the Commission, the NSRF was approved on 18 June 2007; the operational programme for Strengthening Regional Development Potentials and the operational programme for Environmental and Transport Infrastructure Development were approved on 27 August 2007; and the operational programme for Human Resources Development was approved on 21 November 2007.

Towards multi-level governance?

The pre-accession experience of EU funding in Slovenia was a period of learning, when the EU had strong influence at all stages of cohesion policy: it involved a process of developing the appropriate capacities and capabilities at the national level. There was little required by the EU in terms of structures and processes of multi-level governance and little developed. Our interviewees reported that the strategic documents submitted for the 1998–2004 period were authored by the central government, with very little input from actors at other levels or from other sectors (see also Faro 2004).

In theory, sub-national actors would be actively involved in the implementation of projects from these strategic documents, but in practice this involvement was highly variable. In some cases, sub-national actors lacked the capacity to perform their official role and were sidelined by the Commission and central-level institutions (Lajh 2004, 28).

In the pre-accession period the Commission (DG Enlargement) favoured some regionalization but then changed its position as accession drew closer and sought to ensure absorption of the funds centrally. However, in this period Slovenia had prepared regional development plans and pilot regions, which were rejected by the Commission. The Commission's position changed post-accession, with DG Regio the responsible directorate keen to promote *regional* development and accepting of Slovenian arguments. Despite this, in the post-accession period Slovenia has maintained a centralized and state-dominated approach to the management of the structural and cohesion funds.

The vertical dimension

It would be tempting to argue that EU accession has promoted the vertical dimension of multi-level governance in Slovenia through the creation of the two NUTS 2 regions in 2005. However, this development was the outcome of a rational strategic calculation by the central government, which, after repeated attempts, managed to alter the country territorial division for statistical purposes in spite of the Commission's preferences in order to maximize EU funding in the not-so-near future. To use the terminology provided in the opening contribution to this volume (Bache 2010), this is clearly a case of 'thin learning'.

Regarding cohesion policy per se, there was a consensus among our interviewees that cohesion policy-making in the domestic arena is highly centralized and that the main participants in the field are ministries. This applies to both planning and implementation stages. All respondents strongly agreed that GORP was influential over cohesion policy. On the other hand, as GORP is not controlled by the leading party of the coalition government,[12] it has been argued that there is more room for communication and consultations with other policy actors than would have been the case if it was located at the locus of political power (GORP official, interview 2009).

Other important ministries are the Ministry of Economy, Ministry for High Education, Ministry of Environment and Spatial Planning, Ministry for Transport, Ministry for Culture (to a limited extent), Ministry for Finance (as paying authority) and the Office for Budget Controlling (responsible for spending control). Not all interviewees identified the RDAs as influential in the policy process, although some did, while no interviewees mentioned municipalities as important players. However, there is engagement between national and sub-national actors both in planning and implementation.

As noted above, consultations for the SPD for 2004–2006 took place in all Slovene NUTS 3 regions, involving the local authorities, RDAs and various other actors organized at the sub-national level (professional and economic associations, NGOs, social partners, etc.). Moreover, the RDAs were said to be given 'special attention' in these consultations as the bodies that had been responsible for the previous three years for the preparation of the regional development plans, which also had to be prepared in accordance with the partnership principle.

In the process of drawing up the NSRF, the government described partnership with the representatives of RDAs and municipalities as 'an important element of cooperation' (GORP 2007, 9). In this process, a conference was held in July 2006 specifically for engaging with sub-national actors, chaired by the minister responsible for local self-government and regional policy. At this conference and at subsequent meetings, regional and local representatives argued for a 'bottom-up' approach to the implementation of development initiatives and that these should cover 'the widest scope of activities possible (without excessive limitations of the state)' (GORP 2007, 9).

Yet despite the RDAs being involved in consultation processes, they remained weak players within both planning and implementation processes. As one development agency official put it:

> Regional development agencies were established with the goal to decentralize decision-making. But on the other hand, state did not implement its decision to decentralize decision-making. The state was always so strong a negotiator that regional development agencies had left quite limited possibilities for decision-making and participation. Decisions were mainly taken on high policy levels, with no place left for the regional and local level. (Local Development Agency of Ptuj, interview 2008)

The situation in relation to the influence of sub-national actors had not improved under the implementation of the financial perspective 2007–2013, but its nature had changed somewhat. Interviewees reported that the participation of regional-level actors had been squeezed at the expense of the municipalities, which meant that 'the problem is now in the weakness of the small municipalities and lack of regional perspectives' (Ministry of Environment and Spatial Planning (MESP) official, interview 2008). This development was ascribed to the greater political strength of the municipalities, which, unlike the regional bodies, were represented by elected mayors with connections to national political figures.

The horizontal dimension

Much of the emphasis on actor coordination and partnership in Slovenia has focused on the relationships between central ministries rather than between central government and other actors, whether non-state or sub-national. As we have noted above, there was very little pressure from the Commission to develop and implement policies through partnership in the early pre-accession phase, but these requirements grew over time and the impact of this change is evident in the documents prepared for 2004–2006 and 2007–2013, respectively.

It is interesting that in the SPD for 2004–2006, the discussion of partnership refers first to 'close cooperation and consultation by line ministries' (GOSP 2003, 17). When the discussion turns to other actors, it is evident that the approach to consultation varied between ministries responsible for different funds and the overall impact of these consultations on the document delivered to the Commission was marginal. As the SPD itself put it: 'Suggestions and remarks of partners were examined and, where appropriate, included in the SPD' (GOSP 2003, 17). Central government ministries kept a tight grip on the process and the eventual policies contained in the document.

In the NSRF document, there is a significantly more substantial discussion of partnership, reflecting a significantly more substantial degree of engagement between central government and actors beyond the central state. Moreover, the discussion of partnership went beyond engagement for the document itself and built the principle into the implementation, monitoring and evaluation of the NSRF. Of course, wording in documents is one thing, the practical implementation of policy wording quite another. Our research on Slovenia indicated that there had been an increase in cross-sectoral participation over the period of engagement with EU funding and particularly post-accession. However, central government ministries shaped the nature of engagement and continued to exercise influence over key decisions.

The dominance of central government is recognized by civil servants. One Ministry of Environment and Spatial Planning official reported:

> the situation has improved: participation has increased. But the participation system is from the side of decision-makers oriented too much to just formal satisfaction of participation obligations and not to raise quality with participation. The participation process should be used more to improve the quality of decisions. (Interview 2008)

Frustration with the selectivity of central government towards other partners was expressed by a number of non-state actors. For example, one representative of the business community stated that the Ministry of Economy had invited their contribution and proposals had been developed: 'but then in the last six months, three people changed in the ministry and the comments were not considered' (Business Incubator of Pomurje Region official, interview 2008). However, there was also suggestion that a learning process was taking place within government, as suggested by the Ministry of Environment and Spatial Planning official quoted above. Further, a Chamber of Commerce representative (interview 2008) told us that 'in the last year there has been more cooperation because the ministries found out that decisions are not the best quality if only accepted by them'.

Monitoring committees existed for all programmes in Slovenia, as required under EU rules, with representation of a wide range of partners. For Objective 1, there are two monitoring committees, one for the operational programme for Human Resources Development and one for the other two programmes (Strengthening Regional Development Potentials and Environmental and Transport Infrastructure Development). Unsurprisingly, in both cases, the representatives of central government predominate.[13]

In both cases, the influence of the wider partnership was limited, with one GORP official (interview 2009) suggesting that some partners were very unhappy with their level of influence. NGOs felt they were under-resourced and not fully able to partici-pate in either planning or the preparation of projects and were arguing for funding to provide them with technical support to allow them to play a fuller role. As things stood, the resources of central government – whose officials chaired and administered the committees – far outweighed those of other partners, not only in relation to finance but also knowledge and human resources.

Despite Slovenia's position as one of the more compound polities of the Southeast Europe, its adjustment to the governing requirements of EU cohesion policy and related instruments has not been easy. Post-accession, centralization was seen as the most appropriate route for planning and implementing cohesion policy, but even adopting a centralized approach proved far from straightforward. Civil servants inter-viewed reported that the domestic processes were initially too complex and that a more simple modification of pre-accession processes would have been more suitable.

The ensuing lack of efficiency, complicated by political and administrative changes, has led to a rapidly changing and policy framework, but one in which actors beyond central government have been either excluded or engaged at the margins. Moreover, despite ongoing centralization, the process is widely viewed by participants as being slow and bureaucratic. A major issue in terms of effective administration was what was described as a 'big drain of people to other jobs', which limited institutional learning:

> Knowledge is weakened by big fluctuation of people, there are just very few persons in the ministries who stayed on the same posts for long enough time from beginning – to learn and to transfer the knowledge. The most important is learning from doing and the transfer of knowledge from person to person in the working posts. (Ministry of Economy official, interview 2008)

On this point, the government official identified the relatively low salary levels in the public sector as a problem, with civil servants often leaving to take jobs in the private sector. In addition, a number of interviewees emphasized the importance of politics in shaping influence over the funds. One GORP official (interview 2008) reported that when power shifts within the governing coalition, there tends to be a change in the implementation system. At the local level, it was suggested that 'if the mayor of a municipality is in the right party, the possibilities to get funds are higher' (Business Incubator of Pomurje Region official, interview 2008).

More generally, the shift in representation and participation from the regional to the local level under the 2007–2013 programme was also ascribed to party politics by interviewees (as discussed above). However, there was evidence in the recent past of recognition in some central ministries at least that policy effectiveness required both more effective coordination between central ministries and more effective consultation and partnership processes.

Conclusion

Slovenia is an exceptional case among the 2004 entrants to the EU because of its strong corporatist tradition. This tradition, superficially at least, would appear to provide a good fit with the EU's partnership requirement. However, the superficiality of this fit is revealed upon closer examination. The corporatist tradition generally facilitated the participation of limited number of non-state actors (mainly the social partners) in a limited number of policy spheres. In relation to cohesion policy, central ministries were slow to engage widely and tended to view the main coordination challenges as internal to government. The pressures from the EU to engage more widely and more effectively have been slow to impact. It would be thus plausible to deduce that, so far, the main contribution of cohesion policy on state structures and functions is the gradual and selective Europeanization of central government and administration.

In the pre-accession period, the EU gave mixed signals on these issues, defaulting to a support for heavy centralization where the broader goal of enlargement was a priority. Post-accession, DG Regio has been more committed to seeing the multi-level and cross-sectoral aspects of partnership implemented more genuinely. However, the result to date has been the development of a weak system of multi-level governance for cohesion policy in Slovenia, in which the necessary structures and processes have been established to meet the letter of EU requirements, but which do not operate in the spirit of partnership.

Territorial change has certainly been induced by EU cohesion policy – in the form of RDAs at the NUTS 3 level and of the two new NUTS 2 regions established one year after accession. However, domestic moves to introduce provinces – if they are finally approved – appear to offer more promise for the emergence of new Type I multi-level governance bodies at the sub-national level. In short, while the effects of EU cohesion policy are still in their relative infancy, their effects to date have been marginal on the nature of a polity that already has some compound characteristics, but whose predominant characteristic is centralism.

Acknowledgements

This study draws on research funded by the UK Economic and Social Research Council (Multi-level Governance in Southeast Europe, ESRC grant no. RES-062-23-0183). We would like to thank the ESRC for its support and the two anonymous referees for the journal for their helpful comments. All the usual disclaimers apply.

Notes

1. Between January 2008 and July 2009, 17 semi-structured interviews were conducted with representatives of the following organizations: GORP; Government Office for Development; Ministry of Finance; Ministry of Economy; MESP; Chamber of Commerce of Slovenia; Maribor Regional Development Agency (MRA); Local Development Agency of Ptuj (SRC Bistra Ptuj); Business Incubator of Pomurje Region; University of Maribor, Faculty of Economics; the European Commission Directorate General for Enlargement; the European Commission Directorate General for Regional Policy. The interviews were conducted at the last phase of a fieldwork process, following analysis of a range of primary and secondary documents. Interviews were conducted on the basis of individual anonymity and confidentiality with the aid of a semi-structured questionnaire with a mix of closed and open questions.

2. Slovenia was transformed from a one-party (albeit liberalized) communist regime to multi-party democracy, from being a part of Yugoslavia to being an independent country and from having a semi-marketized socialist economy to free social-market economy (Bebler 2002, 127).

3. The NUTS acronym originated from the French *nomenclature des unités territoriales statistiques*. The NUTS system provides a hierarchical categorization of different territorial units in the EU according to five levels, the largest being NUTS 1 (sections of a country grouping together basic regions). This level was subdivided into NUTS 2 (basic regions), with subdivisions continuing through NUTS 3 and NUTS 4 to the smallest level of NUTS 5 (villages and towns). NUTS 2 regions, which were generally defined by member states for their own

regional policy purposes, were the ones adopted for the main territorial objectives of cohesion policy. For practical reasons – that is the availability of suitable data – the NUTS categories were generally based on the existing institutional divisions within member states.
4. The – considerable – influence of workers' councils can be traced back to the Yugoslav system of self-management. In 1993, the system was transformed into a system of councils modelled on the example of German *Betriebsräte*.
5. This subsection draws heavily on European Policies Research Centre (2008, 2–4).
6. Only the comparatively miniscule OPs under the Territorial Cooperation Objective are not under the complete control of GORP.
7. Among the 12 RDAs, three were newly established, five were created from an existing organizational authority (mostly regional entrepreneurial centres) and four were 'networked' RDAs, made up of different organizational authorities with different sectoral agendas.
8. At the earlier stages of the accession negotiations, the Commission had strongly urged the governments of the candidate counties to create elected regional institutions with financial and legal autonomy (Brusis 1999, 23–4).
9. Eastern Slovenia includes the NUTS 3 regions of Pomurska, Podravska, Koroška, Savinjska, Spodnjeposavska, Zasavska, Southeastern Slovenia and Notranjsko-kraška. Western Slovenia includes the NUTS 3 regions of Central Slovenia, Gorenjska, Goriška and Costal-Karst.
10. The new regions were determined with a government resolution (83rd regular session of the government of RS, 54910-3/2005/12, 7 November 2005). The government then filed a motion to the Commission on their notification as NUTS 2 regions.
11. These bodies were: the Ministry of Economy, the Ministry of Environment and Spatial Planning, the Ministry of Education and Sports, Science and Technology, the Ministry of Culture, the Ministry of Agriculture, Forestry and Food, the Ministry of Labour, Family and Social Affairs, the Ministry of Public Administration, the Ministry of Health, the Ministry of Finance, the Ministry of Justice, the Office of the Government of Republic of Slovenia for Macroeconomic Policy and Development, the Government Office for Development, the Government Office for European Affairs, the Office of the Prime Minister of the Republic of Slovenia.
12. Under the last two governments, the minister responsible for GOSP does not come from the leading party. In 2004–2006, he was from the Slovene People's Party, while the leading party was the Slovenian Democratic Party; under the current government, led by the Social Democrats, she is from the Democratic Party of Retired Persons.
13. The members of the monitoring committee of the programme Strengthening Regional Development Potentials and the programme Environmental and Transport Infrastructure Development are representatives of ministries, government offices and departments (18 members); economic and social partners (seven members); NGOs (four members); local governments (four members) and disabled persons (one member). The members of the MC for the programme Human Resources Development are representatives of ministries, government offices and departments (19 members); economic and social partners (seven members); NGOs (three members); local governments (four members) and disabled persons (one member).

References

Bache, I. 2010. Europeanization and multi-level governance: EU cohesion policy and pre-accession aid in Southeast Europe. *Southeast European and Black Sea Studies* 10, no. 1: 1–12.
Bebler, A. 2002. Slovenia's smooth transition. *Journal of Democracy* 13, no. 1: 127–40.
Brusis, M. 1999. Institution building for regional development: A comparison of Bulgaria, the Czech Republic, Estonia, Hungary, Poland and Slovakia. In *Central and Eastern Europe on the way to the European Union: Reforms in Bulgaria, the Czech Republic, Estonia, Hungary, Poland and Slovakia*, ed. E. von Breska and M. Brusis, 1–30. Munich: Centre for Applied Policy Research.
Buchen, C. 2005. East European antipodes: Varieties of capitalism in Estonia and Slovenia. Paper presented at the conference on Varieties of Capitalism in Post-communist Countries, September 23–24, in Paisley University, UK.

European Policies Research Centre. 2008. *Ex post evaluation of cohesion policy programmes 2000–2006 co-financed by ERDF: Working package 11 – Task 1: Overview of management and implementation systems of cohesion policy in 2004–2006; Slovenia.* Glasgow: University of Strathclyde. http://ec.europa.eu/regional_policy/sources/docgener/evaluation/pdf/expost2006/wp11_tsk1_nationa_mis_062000_2.zip.

Faro, J. 2004. Europeanization as regionalisation: Forecasting the impact of EU regional policy export upon the governance structure of Slovenia. Paper presented at Harvard University, Cambridge, MA.

Feldmann, M. 2007. The origins of varieties of capitalism: Lessons from post-socialist transition in Estonia and Slovenia. In *Beyond varieties of capitalism*, ed. B. Hancké, M. Rhodes, and M. Thatcher, 328–52. Oxford: Oxford Scholarship Online Monographs.

GORP (Government Office for Local Self-Government and Regional Policy). 2007. *Slovenia national strategic reference framework 2007–2013, March.* http://www.svlr.gov.si/fileadmin/svlsrp.gov.si/pageuploads/KOHEZIJA/Programski_dokumenti/NSRF_Slovenia_18_06_07_Unoff_eng_trasl.pdf.

GOSP (Government Office for Structural Policies and Regional Development). 2003. *Slovenia single programming document 2004–2006, December.* http://euskladi.gov.si/skladi/1raz/6/single_programming_document_2004-2006_for_slovenia.pdf.

Kovac, Z. 2007. Building a governance framework that enables the establishment of partnerships in Slovenia: Comparison with Ireland and Finland. In *Local innovations for growth in Central and Eastern Europe*, ed. Sylvain Giguère, chap. 4. Paris: OECD Local Economic and Employment Development (LEED) Programme, OECD. (Also in OECD *Social Issues/Migration/Health* 22: 93–118)

Lajh, D. 2004. Europeanisation and regionalisation: Domestic change(s) and structural networks in Slovenia. Paper presented at the ECPR 2004 joint sessions of workshops, Workshop 25 – Policy Networks in Sub-national Governance: Understanding Power Relations, April 14–18, in Uppsala.

Lindstrom, N. 2005. Europeanization and sub-national governance in Slovenia. Paper presented at the ECPR joint sessions of workshops on Societal Regionalism in Western and Eastern Europe, April 15–19, in Granada. http://n.r.lindstrom.googlepages.com/LindstrompaperSlovenia.pdf.

The Europeanization of Bulgarian regional policy: a case of strengthened centralization

Alexander Yanakiev

Department of Politics, University of Sheffield

The study considers whether EU cohesion policy and related pre-accession instruments have contributed to the development of a more compound polity in Bulgaria and promoted features of multi-level governance. In order to examine the impact of the EU cohesion policy on the Bulgarian system of domestic governance, this contribution studies the nature and the extent of domestic change and attempts to trace its causes. The main finding is that Bulgaria's involvement with the EU has led to the creation of a weak system of multi-level governance dominated by the central government. However, it would be premature to jump to any definitive conclusions before the end of the current programming period.

Introduction

This study employs a rationalist approach towards Europeanization (see Bache 2010) in order to explain the changes in the Bulgarian system of governance brought by the preparations to implement the EU cohesion policy that took place in the period preceding the Bulgarian accession to the EU.[1] At least when it comes to Bulgaria (and especially to the EU cohesion policy), a rationalist approach towards the modelling of the effects generated by the EU policies during the pre-accession period is much more appropriate than an approach based on deep learning and socialization, since most of the changes performed in Bulgaria during the pre-accession period were motivated by the expectation for a particular 'reward' from the EU (Schimmelfennig and Sedelmeier 2005).

Rewards varied from increased cooperation and start of the membership negotiations between Bulgaria and the EU (including funding under the pre-accession financial instruments) to full membership of Bulgaria and access to the EU structural funds. When it comes to the changes required if Bulgaria wanted to get the rewards described above, it must be noted that prior to the country's involvement with the EU, Bulgaria was a heavily centralized country, where development efforts were oriented towards the sectors of economy, not towards the territory. From the point of view of the Europeanization concept, this meant that huge adaptation pressures were to be expected and the country had to perform radical transformations of its system of governance.[2] These transformations as well as the 'starting point' (the nature of governance prior to the involvement with the EU) are explained below.

Governance and politics in Bulgaria

Both during the beginning of the pre-accession period and during the first two years of the EU membership, the Bulgarian system of governance was extremely close to the description of simple polities given by the literature (see Bache 2010). The modern Bulgarian state reappeared on the political map of Europe in March 1878 after the last nineteenth-century war between Russia and the Ottoman Empire. Ever since then the country has had a heavily centralized system of governance.

The constitution of the new state adopted in 1879 created a simple system of governance. Policies were adopted by the central government on the basis of the legislation adopted by the Parliament and the monarch acted as a head of state and exercised control over the government, the Parliament and the central government. The powers of the regional governments (appointed by the central government) were limited to the implementation of nationally adopted policies on the governed territory. The new constitution divided the country into 21 territorial administrative units called *okrazia* and 58 *okolii*.

The first administrative reform of Bulgaria took place in 1887, two years after the country united with the former autonomous region of Eastern Rumelia. The country was divided into 26 *okrags* and 84 *okolias*. Although the system saw several changes in 1880s, after the First World War and during the military coups in 1930s, it continued to exist between 1878 and 1947 (Ministry of Regional Development 2006).

The first communist constitution (adopted in 1947) further increased central government control over the policy-formulation process. Even though the two constitutions adopted during the communist regime formally proclaimed the right of self-government for the local administrative units (i.e. the municipalities), no such thing happened in practice. The local authorities continued to have no other powers besides the implementation of the policies formulated by the communist party and most of the non-state actors were liquidated. The system had two veto points (see Risse, Cowles, and Caporaso 2001) – an internal one and an external one. The internal veto point was the Bulgarian Communist Party and the external veto point was the Communist Party of the Soviet Union.

The 1991 Constitution of Republic of Bulgaria (adopted two years after the fall of the communist regime) declared Bulgaria a parliamentary republic and once again gave the powers for policy formulation to the central government. Even though the constitution proclaimed the right of the citizens and the local authorities to unite and the assistance of foreign donors (i.e. USAID, British Know-how Fund, etc.) resulted in the creation of a multitude of civil society organizations (22,366 between 1995 and 2005), most of these assumed the role of passive beneficiaries of donor assistance and failed to empower their target groups to take part in the decision-making process (Dorosiev and Ganev 2008). Prior to the beginning of the Bulgarian involvement with the EU (1997), the role of the local authorities was to provide public services to the population and to implement policies that were adopted by the central government and the Parliament.

Although widely proclaimed as 'people's democratic rule', communism only contributed to the strengthening of centralism. The Bulgarian political and organizational culture after the end of communism was also dominated by centralism, even though there were many more channels of participation of the actors outside the central government than during the time of the Bulgarian kingdom or communism. According to the 1991 Bulgarian Constitution, the process of policy formulation is taking place mostly within the central government. The central government also controls the policy implementation process.

Following the 1999–2001 administrative reform, most of the ministries dating from the communist period (i.e. the Ministry of Trade and the Ministry of Foreign Economic Relations) were either reformed and unified into 'mega ministries' (the Ministry of Economy and the Ministry of Transport and Communications) or saw their administration and functions significantly reduced and transferred to the newly formed policy implementation agencies (these were still under the control of the respective ministers).[3]

Currently, the country is governed by more than 20 ministries and national-level policy implementation agencies. Each of these is responsible for a specific policy sector and acts as a centre of the policy network formed around the related policy area. The donor-driven process of creation of civil society organizations made these organizations dependent on external aid. As a result, only a limited number of civil society organizations managed to gain a degree of financial independence and the political culture remained under the dominance of centralism.

Policy goals as a catalyst of change

It would be all but impossible to attribute any of the changes brought by the implementation of the EU pre-accession support instruments and the preparation for implementation of the EU cohesion policy to the preferences of domestic actors (be it the Bulgarian central government, the local authorities or the non-state actors). Practically, all of the changes in Bulgarian governance that happened during the pre-accession period can be attributed to the process of the 'return to the European Family'.

This process began in the beginning of 1990s following the collapse of the communist regime in November of 1989. If viewed from a policy goal perspective, it represents a multitude of strategic policy goals related to the transition from the communist regime and the central planned economy to a liberal democracy and market economy. In order to deliver on these policy goals, the new Bulgarian governments had to undertake radical administrative, economic and political reforms (for which there was no ready model), as well as to gain access to new markets (given the loss of the vast market of the Soviet Union). At that time, the EU provided both the only available policy model and the only available market.

Bulgaria and the EU

Although Bulgaria established diplomatic relations with the European Economic Community in 1988, these relations began to develop more significantly after the fall of the communist regime with the conclusion of a Partnership and Association Agreement (also known as a European Agreement) with the European communities in April 1993. According to the scarce Bulgarian literature covering this period, the main goal of the European Agreement (besides trade liberalization) was the gradual introduction of the associated country to the principles of the Common Market (Kuneva 2007). In fact, besides liberalization, the European Agreement covered most of the areas that were later (in 2000) to become the accession negotiation chapters.

As far as regional policy is concerned, the European Agreement contained provisions for the exchange of information between the national, regional and local authorities and the provision of specific assistance to Bulgaria in order for the latter to formulate its own regional policy (Article 88 of the European Agreement). After 1999, such assistance was being delivered in the framework of Phare programme. From a conceptual point of view, at this point the relations between the EU and Bulgaria were not determined by the accession conditionality, and the Europeanization of the Bulgarian regional development policy can be explained by social learning (Schimmelfennig and Sedelmeier 2005; Bache 2010).

Besides the lack of accession conditionality, there were also several reasons for the appropriateness of the social learning model. First of all, like the other Central and Eastern European Country (CEEC) applicants, Bulgaria had to undergo significant reforms, such as finding a replacement for the sectoral approach to the economic development (which was clearly not working in the beginning of 1990s) and address-ing the steadily growing regional disparities within the country. In order to start such reforms, the Bulgarian governments needed an easily adaptable external model of liberal democracy and market economy. Second, besides a model for such reforms, the EU also provided assistance (both expert and financial) for these reforms. Third, the motivation provided by the European Agreement was the possibility for Bulgarian businesses to gain partial access to the Common Market.

The European Agreement came into force in 1995. In December 1995, following an increasing internal pressure for the integration of the country into the 'Euro-Atlantic family' (in other words for the submission of applications for membership into EU and NATO), the socialist government managed to secure a parliamentary approval and submitted the official application of the Republic of Bulgaria for EU membership. During the whole of 1996 and the first half of 1997, the country went into a severe economic and political crisis and opening membership negotiations became impossible. The country had already stabilized its economy and a new right-wing government came to power, when the Commission published its Opinion on Bulgaria's readiness for EU membership in July 1997. Like the Opinions on the other CEECs, the Opinion on Bulgaria was structured according to the Copenhagen Criteria. The country was evaluated according to political criteria, economic criteria and the ability to take obligations of membership.

Regional policy fell within the scope of economic criteria. Since the main goals of the EU cohesion policy are economic growth and prosperity, the section on regional policy and cohesion in the Opinion on Bulgaria contained some brief statistics about the overall economic situation in the country, describing the increasing regional disparities within the country due to the decline of the industry and agriculture (partially caused by the Land reform). When it came to policy-making, the Opinion identified a major 'misfit' (below) between Bulgaria and the EU level; the country was practically being evaluated as having no regional policy. According to the Commission, most of the regional development initiatives in Bulgaria were imple-mented within the framework of a sectoral approach.

As far as the institutional misfits between Bulgaria and the EU were concerned, the Opinion was extremely brief, citing that Bulgaria lacked the proper administrative framework for a regional development policy. The section finished by recommending the strengthening of the administrative procedures and the establishment of inter-ministerial coordination (European Commission 1997). The Luxemburg European Council (December 1997) included Bulgaria in the procedure according to Article 49 of the Treaty on European Union (membership in the EU) and decided that the accession negotiations with Bulgaria 'will begin when substantial progress on the implementation of the membership criteria is achieved' (Kuneva 2007). Accession negotiations between Bulgaria and the EU started in 2000 and lasted until the end of 2006.

Pre-requisites for change

From the point of view of the Europeanization literature, the national-level changes in response to the adaptation pressures depend on the degree of fit between the national-level policies and practices and the respective EU policies and practices (see Bache 2010). The greater the misfit between the national and the EU levels, the greater the expected domestic change. However, according to Börzel and Risse (2003), the misfit is a necessary but not a sufficient requirement if one is expected to see domestic change in response to the adaptation pressures from the EU. Besides the degree of misfit, the following mediating factors influence the process of domestic change.

Mediating formal institutions

In the case of Bulgaria, there was a single group of interconnected formal institutions that were able to facilitate the transformation of the EU adaptation pressures into domestic change. This group consisted of the institutions of central government. Central government institutions were the only ones able to receive the information about particular misfits between the national and the EU levels and carry out the domestic change required in order to improve the degree of fit.

Multiple veto points

According to Börzel and Risse (2003, 57), the existence of multiple veto points in the country's governance architecture can block or delay domestic changes in response to EU adaptation pressures. The Bulgarian system of governance has two major potential veto points – the Ministry of Finance and the Parliament.

The origin of the veto powers of the Bulgarian Parliament lies within its competences to adopt new legislation and control the central government. The changes in the national institutional framework and the procedures for the implementation of new policies (including the ones related to EU-level policies) have to be governed by the appropriate legislation. This was especially the case during the pre-accession period when even the direct effect *acquis* had to be transposed. Therefore, the Parliament had the scope to radically influence the implementation of a new policy or even block the introduction of such policy.

However, from 1995 the Bulgarian central governments were backed by stable parliamentary majorities, with all prime ministers but four being the leaders of the political party with the most seats in the Parliament. As a result, no policy initiatives were blocked, even though heated and often lengthy debates frequently delayed reforms that were a response to the EU adaptation pressures (for example, the constitutional amendments related to the status of the MPs and the judicial system were adopted at the very last moment in 2006). On the other hand, the source of veto powers of the Ministry of Finance lies within its budget drafting and public expenditure management competencies.

Political and organizational culture

From 1878, the Bulgarian political and organizational culture has been built on the basis of centralism. Prior to 1944, the most important element of this culture was the dominating role of the central government and the monarch. Even in the 1930s, when the country was practically ruled by the monarch, changes were always initiated and carried out by the central government.

The reason for this was related to the fact that the key issue for the newly emerged Bulgarian state between 1878 and the late 1940s was national unification. In an attempt to achieve unification of all lands populated by Bulgarians under the reign of the Bulgarian monarchs, the country fought three wars with its neighbours and took an active part in the First World War. The successful completion of the national unification project required a strong central government and left little room for the parliamentary opposition and non-state actors to take any part in national decision-making processes.

The main cohesion policies and instruments

The Phare programme, created in 1989 in order to assist the economic reconstruction of Poland and Hungary after the fall of communism (see Bache 2010), was made available to seven countries including Bulgaria in 2000. From 2000 onwards, Phare was engaged in: (1) capacity and institution building for the implementation of the *acquis communautaire* and for overcoming the structural, sectoral and regional disparities, and (2) the approximation of national and EU quality standards.

Following the accession of Bulgaria to the EU, the funds allocated to the country under Phare were transferred to a Transitional Facility. Phare implementation was managed by four implementing agencies in the Ministry of Regional Development and Public Works, the Ministry of Economy, the Ministry of Labour and Social Policy and the Ministry of Finance. The work of these agencies was controlled by a national aid coordinator and a national authorizing officer. Both posts were occupied by deputy ministers of finance.

The Instrument for Structural Policies for Pre-Accession (ISPA) was created by the EU in June 1999 to assist the 10 acceding countries in achieving the goals set in the Accession Partnership and to strengthen economic and social cohesion in Central and Eastern Europe. In the field of transport in Bulgaria, the programme provided assistance for large-scale infrastructure projects that were part of the trans-European transport network (TEN-T) (such as the Lyulin motorway, the Sofia Airport and the Plovdiv – Svilengrad railway) and for the renewal of the port of Burgas. The programme was managed by five administrative bodies at the Roads Executive Agency, the Ministry of Environment and Waters, the Ministry of Transport and a joint executive agency between the Ministry of Regional Development and the Ministry of Environment and Waters.

Like Phare, the overall coordination of ISPA was within the competencies of the Ministry of Finance. It must be noted that these projects had no effect on the local authorities – excluding their impact on the local economy. Environmental projects funded under the programme, however, were directly related to the services provided by the local authorities, such as waste disposal and water supply. The environmental component of ISPA was jointly managed by the Ministry of Regional Development and the Ministry of Environment. Prior to 2004, the overall budget of the ISPA programme was €1 billion per year for 2000–2006 period. In 2004, the overall budget for the ISPA programme for Bulgaria and Romania was €425 million.[4] ISPA projects in Bulgaria that were not completed prior to 1 January 2007 were transferred to the Cohesion Fund.

The Special Accession Programme for Agricultural and Rural Development (Sapard) was created in 1999 in order to assist the candidate countries for the preparation of their agricultural producers for the Common Agriculture Policy and to promote the planning and implementation of the rural development policies of the candidate countries during 2000–2006. The programme was managed by the Ministry of Agriculture.[5]

As can be inferred from the description of each pre-accession instrument, the direct management of the pre-accession support was organized on the basis of the lead ministry principle. Each of the executive agencies that managed the measure under a particular component of the pre-accession financial instruments (for example institution building under Phare) was usually an administrative unit within the lead ministry, staffed by public officials from the same ministry and directly accountable to the deputy minister in charge of European affairs in the respective ministry.

The nature and the extent of domestic change

Any process of domestic change in Bulgaria in response to the need to 'fit' the national policies into the framework of the EU rules usually passes through three identifiable phases – the identification of misfit, the actual change and the evaluation of change.

Identification of misfits

At this stage, usually the European Commission identified the misfit between the Bulgarian national-level policies and practices related to the regional development and 'pointed them out' to the Bulgarian central government (its main partner in Bulgaria). The misfits were usually identified on the basis of the requirements for the implementation of the EU cohesion policy and pointed out to the Bulgarian government through either formal or informal channels. The formal channels usually included the Regular Reports on Bulgarian progress towards EU membership, the common positions exchanged during the inter-governmental conferences between Bulgaria and the EU, as well as the meetings of various joint sub-committees established under the Association Agreement of 1993. The informal channels usually included the personal contacts of high-ranking Bulgarian public servants with the EU institutions.

Actual change

In the earlier candidacy years, the process of actual change usually began with the 'harmonization' of the respective legislation with the *acquis*. In the case of instruments relating to cohesion policy, however, it is very hard to speak of 'harmonization' of the Bulgarian legislation, since prior to the publishing of the 1997 Opinion of the European Commission, the country had no regional policy and any development programming was done sector-by-sector on an annual basis. Therefore, an entirely new framework legislation (the Law on Regional Development) had to be adopted in order to set up the regionalization of the country in accordance with the NUTS system (see Bache 2010), the programming mechanism and the new institutional framework needed for the implementation of EU cohesion policy.

The new programming mechanism envisaged that the local authorities should prepare plans for the development of the governed territory. The plans were later to be used for the preparation of the NUTS 3 and NUTS 2 level development plans. The regional development plans of the NUTS 2 regions were, in turn, used in order to draft the national regional development operational programme by the Ministry of Regional Development. It must be noted, however, that the NUTS 2 regions in Bulgaria were purely statistical units and were not headed by a specific administration (either appointed by the central government or elected).

The only administrative units that existed on the NUTS 2 level were the regional development councils. These councils met on ad hoc basis in order to approve the NUTS 2 region development plans and to forward them to the central government. Procedures for inter-institutional coordination were then agreed between the cabinet ministries and formally adopted by the central government. Usually during the pre-accession period, partners outside the government (central or local) had a limited say in the process, excluding a number of national-level non-central government organizations such as the National Association of Municipalities.

The evaluation of changes

The name of this phase to a significant extent speaks for itself. During this phase, the central government services usually prepared various reporting documents that were submitted to the European Commission. Once the Commission was satisfied with the changes, the candidate country received an external incentive, such as a praise of its achievements in the next Regular Report and the closing of the respective negotiation chapter, until all negotiation chapters were closed and the candidate country was given the chance to sign an accession agreement.

At least in theory, as a candidate country, Bulgaria should have had no opportunity to upload its preferences to the EU level. However, due to the concerns of the European Commission with the Bulgarian capacity for implementation of the EU regional policy, the solutions adopted during the accession negotiations under Chapter 21 in fact had the effect of a limited uploading of the Bulgarian preferences to the EU level, before the country became an EU member. How did this become possible?

In their study of the regionalization of the candidate countries from the Fifth Enlargement of the EU, Hughes, Sasse, and Gordon (2004) mention that before the completion of the first wave of the Fifth Enlargement, the European Commission changed its approach from building multi-level governance to preparations for effi-cient implementation of the EU cohesion policy in the candidate countries. Needless to say, such efficient implementation required a certain degree of administrative and financial capacity, which was available to the central government. Therefore, it is not surprising that the system for implementation of the EU structural funds in Bulgaria was dominated by the central government.

The changing power of EU conditionality

Schimmelfennig and Sedelmeier (2005, 211) suggest that one should distinguish between the democratic conditionality and the *acquis* conditionality. They use the term 'democratic conditionality' in order to describe the general EU rules of liberal democracy. According to Schimmelfennig and Sedelmeier, 'the EU has applied its conditionality from the very start of the transformations in the CEECs'.

The association agreements between the former communist countries and the EU were such conditionality instruments. The EU democratic conditionality worked together with the efforts of other west European organizations such as the Council of Europe, NATO and the OECD to assist the democratization of eastern Europe. According to Schimmelfennig and Sedelmeier (2005), the main external incentives offered by the democratic conditionality were the institutional links with the EU. However, a brief review on the history of Bulgarian transition towards democracy would show that hardly any change in the former communist countries can be attributed to democratic conditionality.

In fact the changes that Schimmelfennig and Sedelmeier (2005) attributed to democratic conditionality were about to happen with or without the impact of the EU, since the former communist system of governance had to be replaced. The reward offered by democratic conditionality – the institutional links with the EU – was not a sufficient catalyst for a general change of the national system of governance. The creation of institutional links was not a feasible reward for the adoption of the EU rules.

Furthermore, the forging of institutional links between the former communist countries and what was then the EEC actually started during the later years of the communist regimes (around 1988), when most communist countries established diplomatic relations with the EEC itself, besides the pre-existing bilateral relations with the EEC member states. What democratic conditionality offered was a model for the post-communist reforms, a possibility for strengthening the bilateral economic relations, the exchange of practices in various policy sectors and some financial and expert support on behalf of the EU (via the Phare programme). At this point, the adaptation pressures originated mostly from the need to perform a quick transition from a state-controlled to market economy.

The *acquis* conditionality came at a much later stage, when the criteria for EU membership were already formulated and the post-communist countries began to prepare for full membership. At this point, the main external incentive for adoption of the EU rules by the candidate countries was the perspective for a full EU membership. In order to get this reward, the former communist countries had to adopt the EU rules and standards in order to get this reward. From the point of view of the misfit concept, this is when the misfits between the national and the EU levels were identified and the candidate countries began to experience adaptation pressures originating at the EU level. In the case of Bulgaria (as in the other post-communist countries), the *acquis* conditionality began to replace the democratic conditionality in 1997, when the European Commission published its Opinion on Bulgaria's readiness for EU membership.

Tracing the causes of domestic change

Before addressing this point, I would like to shed some light on the type of changes that were needed in Bulgaria in order for the country to prepare for the EU membership. First of all, if any changes were to occur as a result of the country's involvement with the EU, the Union had to have a domestic partner in the bargaining process. Such a partner should have been able to 'keep track' of the requirements that the country should fulfil in order to receive the ultimate external incentive (the full EU membership) and initiate and manage the processes that were to lead to the required changes.

When it came to the implementation of (any) Community policies, the first change needed was the adoption of new legislation. During the pre-accession period, the process was known as 'harmonization' of legislation. It was needed because even though most of the EU legislation related to the common policies were directly applicable in the member states, it was not applicable in Bulgaria at the time when the country began its accession negotiations. A second change that was required was related to the creation of the institutional frameworks that were needed for the implementation of Community policies.

This change also required changes in the legal framework of the candidate country (i.e. in the regulations concerning the civil service), an extensive capacity-building process (usually in the form of establishing training infrastructure and of training a 'critical' mass of civil servants from various levels of government over a limited period of time), the set-up of complicated sets of cooperation procedures between various institutions (aiming at resolving inter-institutional conflicts), as well as the organization of national-level partnerships (i.e. by the drafting of guidelines for the implementation of the partnership principle).

All these reforms usually require the participation of the biggest national-level actor – the central government. The first change provoked by the preparation for the implementation of the EU structural funds was actually in the power relations between the cabinet ministries within the central government. During the communist regime, the most powerful cabinet ministries (excluding the ministries of defence and interior[6]) were usually the ones that were in charge of the heavy industry and the foreign trade. Partially as a result of the adaptation pressures of the administrative criteria for membership, during shortly before and immediately after the beginning of the accession negotiations with the EU (1999–2000), the cabinet ministries overseeing the foreign trade and the heavy industry became a part of the newly formed mega-cabinet ministry called the Ministry of Economy.

During the communist regime, cabinet ministries such as Finance played a secondary role, cabinet ministries such as the Regional Development had completely different working sectors and cabinet ministries such as Environment and Waters had not even existed as an independent ministry. However, the perspective for EU pre-accession support and the accession negotiations under the *acquis* chapters with financial implications (regional policy and structural instruments and agriculture) significantly changed the role of the Ministry of Finance. One of the first require-ments of the European Commission was that a special unit for central management of the EU pre-accession funds should be set up; such a unit was set up within the minis-try. By 2002, the ministry already had the overall responsibility for the coordination of Community support and the implementation of the strategic planning documents related to the EU structural funds and retained this responsibility until the summer of 2008, when a special deputy prime minister was appointed to manage the EU structural funds.

However, the ministry remained one of the most powerful ministries, since the deputy prime minister had to be supported by the staff of the Ministry of Finance. From the point of view of this research, this realignment of the cabinet ministries and the concentration of the overall control over the EU regional policy in the hands of one ministry meant strong central government control over the regional policy imple-mentation and confirmed the existence of a strong vertical dimension dominated by one partner (the central government) in the Bulgarian regional policy implementation architecture.

Another important change was that, as a result of the Opinion of the European Commission, Bulgaria was forced to formulate its own regional policy in order to receive the external incentives offered by the EU during the accession negotiations. However, since the *acquis* related to EU regional policy contained no detailed requirements about the institutional structure, the Bulgarian government managed to impose a centralized system for the EU regional policy implementation in Bulgaria.

When it comes to the local authorities, the changes provoked by the preparation for implementation of the EU regional policy were not that visible as in the case of the central government. In fact, even after a very detailed look, one might safely assume that when it comes to the local authorities, there was limited (if any) change, despite the adaptation pressures from Brussels, originating from central government and from the fact that the Bulgarian local authorities had been offered tangible external incentives – contributions from the pre-accession financial instruments and the EU structural funds towards the development of the governed territory.

Like the central government, the Bulgarian local authorities started to experience the first adaptation pressures related to the implementation of the EU regional policy shortly after the European Commission published its Opinion on Bulgarian readiness for EU membership in 1997. The 1999 Law on Regional Development and two subsequent laws (2004, 2008; National Assembly of Republic of Bulgaria 1999, 2004, 2008) – adopted in response to the adaptation pressures coming from the EU – required the local authorities to take active part in the programming and implementation of the EU regional policy.

However, the laws set no requirements for the creation of a local administrative framework for dealing with the programming process on local level. Moreover, due to the long-term culture of financial and capacity dependence on the central government, only a handful of local authorities (the largest ones) managed to invest in the creation of their own programming capacity. Most local governments relied on central government to help them with capacity building and to intervene in order to correct errors in the programming process at local level.

Bulgarian involvement with the EU also gave the local authorities the opportunity to establish contacts with local authorities from other member states in order to defend joint interests in the European institutions. Again due to lack of capacity, a limited number of local authorities were able to benefit from this opportunity without the help of the national-level associations of local authorities. In fact, one and a half years after Bulgaria became a full member of the EU and 10 months after the Bulgarian strategic documents were negotiated with the European Commission, only two of the biggest Bulgarian cities and the National Association of Municipalities were represented in Brussels and a only handful of others had some contacts with local authorities from the EU15.

The smallest degree of change can be seen in the case of non-state actors. In order to comply with the requirement for implementation of the partnership principle and in order to benefit from the specific knowledge of some non-state actors (i.e. business organizations, environmental organizations, regional development agencies), central government arranged their participation in the drafting of various strategic documents and allowed them to take part in the monitoring committees of the operational programmes. However, the decision-making process in the monitoring committees and similar bodies remained under the control of the state.

If one takes a look at the text of the Ordinance 171/2004 (Bulgarian Council of Ministers; Council of Ministers of Republic of Bulgaria 2002/2004) regulating the formation of the various monitoring bodies, it is easy to see that state control was all but inevitable, since most members of the monitoring bodies represented the central government, and forming a 'government' majority was not a problem even if some of the representatives of the central government decided to take the side of the non-state actors. It appears that the Commission did not actually press for the greater inclusion of the social and economic partners in the decision-making process, despite the occasional mentioning (in the Regular Reports on Bulgarian progress towards EU membership) of this need. Due to the lack of any effective conditionality on the greater participation of the non-state actors, it is highly likely that their participation in the implementation of EU regional policy is going to remain at best limited during the first programming period of the Bulgarian EU membership (2007–2013).

Conclusion

To summarize, the Bulgarian involvement with the EU and the expectations for financial support from EU regional policy during EU membership brought the biggest changes in the realm of the central government. The need to meet the requirements of EU regional policy led to the rearrangement of the institutional framework of the central government and made the Ministry of Finance one of the most influential government departments in Bulgaria.

The role of the central government, local authorities and non-state actors in the Bulgarian system for the implementation of the EU regional policy suggests that the country's involvement with the EU led to the creation of a weak system of multi-level governance, that can be described as a mixture of Type I and Type II. Like the case of Britain (Bache 2008, 28), general purpose jurisdictions (the central government) co-exist with a small number of task-specific jurisdictions such as the National Strategic Reference Framework and various operational programme monitoring committees as well as the regional development agencies.[7]

However, in the case of Bulgaria, the Type I part of the mixture is stronger and the central government dominates the task-specific jurisdictions, because of the limited number of participants outside the central government in these structures. Most of the Type II structures were created at the last stage of the pre-accession period (2006) in order to oversee the implementation of the respective strategic planning documents (national operational programmes); it is therefore still hard to say whether the Type II structures have had any effect on the governance of EU cohesion policy in Bulgaria. Such an effect can be expected to manifest itself around the end of the current programming period (2007–2013), when the country will be in the process of appraising the results of the first structural funds cycle and preparing the strategic planning documents for the next structural funds cycle.

Notes

1. This contribution is based on Ph.D. research conducted at the University of Sheffield. In addition to consulting a broad range of primary and secondary documents, this also involved interviews with 18 policy-makers from a cross-section of organizations involved in cohesion policy and related pre-accession instruments that were conducted in both Brussels and Bulgaria in 1998 and 1999.

2. Here I draw on the two types of multi-level governance developed by Marks and Hooghe (2004; see also Bache 2010). Type I multi-level governance describes system-wide governing arrangements in which the dispersion of authority is restricted to a limited number of clearly defined, non-overlapping jurisdictions at a limited number of territorial levels, each of which has responsibility for a 'bundle' of functions. By contrast, Type II multi-level governance describes governing arrangements in which the jurisdiction of authority is task-specific, where jurisdictions operate at numerous territorial levels and may be overlapping.
3. See the Law on Civil Servant and the Law on Administration, available at http://www.lex.bg (in Bulgarian).
4. For information on the management of ISPA programme see http://minfin.bg/en/page/73.
5. http://www.mzgar.government.bg/Sapard/Sapard.htm.
6. The Ministry of Interior was usually overseeing the work of the respective political police service.
7. The Bulgarian regional development agencies are a form of public–private partnership between the local authorities, the local business, the NGOs and the academia. The goals of these partnerships are to promote the development of the territory they are based on.

References

Bache, I. 2008. *Europeanization and multi-level governance: Cohesion policy in the European Union and Britain.* Lanham, MD: Rowan and Littlefield.

Bache, I. 2010. Europeanization and multi-level governance: EU cohesion policy and pre-accession aid in Southeast Europe. *Southeast European and Black Sea Studies* 10, no. 1: 1–12.

Börzel, T., and T. Risse. 2003. When Europe hits home: Europeanization and domestic change. In *The politics of Europeanization*, ed. C. Radaelli and K. Featherstone, 57–80. Oxford: Oxford University Press.

Council of Ministers of Republic of Bulgaria. 2002/2004. Ordinance 171 on the creation of a Coordination Council for the National Development Plan.

Dorosiev, R., and G. Ganev. 2008. *Bulgaria: 'Countries in transition' report series.* Freedom House Europe. http://www.freedomhouse.hu/index.php?option=com_content&task=view&id=196 (accessed May 2009).

European Commission. 1997. *Opinion of the European Commission on the Bulgarian application for membership.* http://www.evropa.bg (accessed January 2008).

Hughes, J., G. Sasse, and C. Gordon. 2004. *Europeanization and regionalization in the EU's enlargement to Central and Eastern Europe: The myth of conditionality.* Basingstoke: Palgrave Macmillan.

Kuneva, M. 2007. *Европа на Гражданите* [Europe of the citizens]. Sofia: Colibri [in Bulgarian].

Marks, G., and L. Hooghe. 2004. Contrasting visions of multi-level governance. In *Multi-level governance*, ed. I. Bache and M. Flinders, 15–30. Oxford: Oxford University Press.

Ministry of Regional Development. 2006. *Historical development of the administrative subdivision of Republic of Bulgaria* [in Bulgarian]. http://www.mrrb.government.bg.

National Assembly of Republic of Bulgaria. 1999, 2004, 2008. Law on regional development.

Risse, T., M. Cowles, and J. Caporaso. 2001. Europeanization and domestic change. In *Europeanization and domestic change: Transforming Europe*, ed. M. Cowles, J. Caporaso, and T. Risse, 1–20. Ithaca, NY: Cornell University Press.

Schimmelfennig, F., and U. Sedelmeier. 2005. *The Europeanization of Central and Eastern Europe* (Cornell Studies in Political Economy). Ithaca, NY: Cornell University Press.

Europeanization and new patterns of multi-level governance in Romania

Ana Maria Dobre

Faculty of Social Sciences, University of Leuven, Leuven, Belgium

Europeanization and new patterns of multi-level governance in Romania

Ana Maria Dobre

Faculty of Social Sciences, University of Leuven, Leuven, Belgium

This study considers whether EU cohesion policy and related pre-accession instruments have contributed to the development of a more compound polity in Romania and, specifically, considers the extent to which there is a process of Europeanization characterized by emergent features of multi-level governance. In particular, it brings forward a number of explanatory factors which account for the process of regions' creation in a centralized unitary post-communist state such as Romania. It shows that the regional reforms and regionalization have occurred in a very functional way and mostly as a means of accessing and managing regional-level structural funds. It concludes by illustrating the emergence of new patterns of multi-level governance in the context of socialization and engagement with the EU's cohesion policy.

Introduction

This study analyses the governance effects of EU's cohesion policy in Romania and considers whether this has created a more compound polity. In particular, it focuses on the emergence of the phenomenon of the institutionalization of regions. The study looks mainly at the period from 1990 to 2007, which corresponds to the end of the communist regime, the democratic transition and the EU pre-accession process.[1]

Following this introduction, the second section sets out the context of politics in Romania and looks at the institutional and governance characteristics of the state organization. The third section presents the external EU conditionality mechanisms. The fourth section examines the domestic response to this framework of EU pressures for membership and presents the institutional and policy changes in the field of territorial and cohesion policy. The fifth section traces the causes of domestic change, specifically discussing the external and domestic sources of change. The concluding section sketches an overall assessment and emphasizes the emergence of multi-level governance patterns in Romania.

Governance and politics in Romania

In the period immediately after the breakdown of communism, Romania could be clearly described as a simple polity according to Schmidt's categorizations (Bache

2010). However, it is suggested here that the EU and domestic drivers have combined to push Romania in a more compound direction.

The dominant state tradition, starting with the nineteenth century, was political, economic and administrative centralization, influenced by the French Jacobinism (Hitchins 1996). Additionally, other state traditions such as historical regionalism have influenced the state organization, since prior to the nineteenth century, the territory was composed of historical regions (Moldavia, Vallachia and Transylvania) with numerous internal regional territorial sub-divisions, which benefited from different degrees of autonomy.

In the period after the communist breakdown, the post-communist decision-makers opted for the re-establishment of the centralized state tradition, influenced by the predominance of centralism throughout the twentieth century, reinforced by more than 40 years of communist rule. This contributed to the adoption, in 1991, of a new constitution, which defined Romania as a 'sovereign, independent, unitary and indivisible Nation State' (Article 1 of the Romanian Constitution).

At the same time, however, post-communist Romania initiated important steps towards the decentralization of the state organization. Based on the 1991 Constitution, a first Act on Local Government institutionalized the current structures of local government, which consist of two layers with legal authority and administrative structures: county and local level (rural communes [*comună*], towns [*oraş*] and municipalities [*municipiu*]) (Law no. 69/1991). All local administrative units have directly elected authorities (Law no. 70/1992 and Law no. 35/2008). County authorities co-exist with *deconcentrated units* of central government.

With regard to economic and fiscal competences, local- and county-level institutions are financed through three categories of revenue: own revenues including local taxes, state transfers and borrowing (Matei et al. 2003, 63–4).

This trend towards substantive local administration reforms was reinforced by the EU requirements in the context of EU membership negotiations. As a consequence, the system was adjusted to meet these requirements, as well as the principles of the European Charter of Local Self-Government (ratified by Romania in 1997): local self-government and decentralization, financial autonomy, eligibility of local authorities, citizens' participation, and the appropriateness and legality of the local authorities' decisions. The 2003 Constitution (Article 120.1) lays down the principles of local governance: 'decentralization, local autonomy and deconcentration of public services'.

More recently, new steps for the strengthening of local self-government have been taken with the adoption, in 2006, of a new Law on Decentralization (Law no. 286/2006). Its positive impact can be seen at different levels: the classification of territorial-administrative units on the basis of their administrative capacity; the delimitation between central, county and local authorities' competencies. Additionally, the central public administrative authorities have not only to consult the local authorities before adopting any decision, but they also cannot impose any responsibility on the local authorities without providing financial support (Local Government and Public Service Reform Initiative 2009).

In terms of institutional democratic expression, Romania is a unitary state characterized by party pluralism, several types of electoral system, artificial bicameralism, strong dual executive and a majoritarian logic system (Morar 2002). The participation of civil society in policy-making processes has been rather weak (Bădescu 2008, 87).

In sum, governance in Romania has gradually evolved throughout the 1990s to the present from a simple polity and a unitary state towards a more compound polity system. The joint effect of domestic state traditions and external factors (the EU and the Council of Europe) has led to changes to the dominant centralist understanding of the state and allowed for two main developments: (1) the introduction of political, administrative and fiscal decentralization combined with trends of local deconcentration, and (2) the emergence of statistical regionalization (Dobre, forthcoming). The following discussion considers the potential effect of EU cohesion policy and pre-accession instruments.

EU cohesion policy and pre-accession instruments

Pre-accession financial assistance for Romania was distributed through three main instruments: Phare, ISPA and Sapard (see Bache 2010). The contribution of pre-accession funds for Romania was: €860 million in 2004, €931 million in 2005 and €1002 million in 2006 (European Commission 2002, 43). This represented a very important financial resource for Romania (around 1.4% of GDP).

In specific terms, the EU financial assistance for Romania related to regional policy, as in the case of the other candidate countries, and was linked both with the need of reducing the regional disparities and economic backwardness of the regions and with the country's capacity to administer the pre- and post-accession funds. In this field, the objective of the Phare budget, which since 1997 has devoted 30% of its total funds to 'institution building' (European Commission 1997), was to prepare Romania for introducing institutions for regional development and for assisting the country to adopt a modern and efficient administration capable of accessing and managing the pre-accession and the structural and cohesion funds.

One of the main elements of financial assistance in the field of regional policy was, for instance, the twinning process. Accordingly, by 2001, 'Romania had benefited from 66 projects (approximately 9 per cent of the total number launched) which have attracted funding of €63.1 million (corresponding to 13.3 per cent of the total twinning budget). Out of these 66 projects, 16 have been in the field of public finance and the internal market, 13 in the field of regional policy, 12 in the JHA field, 10 in the field of agriculture and the remaining 25 divided between other policy areas' (Papadimitriou and Phinnemore 2004, 626).

Additional to the financial framework, the European Commission imposed a series of requirements to be addressed and monitored during the accession negotiations: (1) the legislative framework; (2) the territorial organization (i.e. the NUTS classification for the implementation of structural funds; see Bache 2010); (3) programming capacity (development plans, procedures for multi-annual programming of budgetary expenditure, the implementation of the partnership principle at the different stages of programming, financing, monitoring and evaluation of structural funds assistance); (4) the institutional framework – administrative capacity; and (5) the financial and budgetary management (European Commission 2002).

At the same time, Romania had to fulfil a number of specific EU conditions and requirements in order to prepare for accession in the field of regional policy. Also, the Commission stressed the opening of the internal process of implementation of the partnership principle in the framework of the drafting of the National Development Plan (NDP) 2004–2006. In this framework, the regional and local economic and social partners and the agencies for development were consulted and actively involved in the selection of programmes to be presented to the Commission for financing. In the 2004 Country Progress Report, as in the following Monitoring Country Reports from 2005 (European Commission 2005) and 2006 (European Commission 2006), the Commission put into evidence Romania's adaptation in the legislative and institutional fields, while stressing the need for progress and strengthened internal adaptation in terms of the administrative capacity of the institutional structures, and in the areas of financial management and control, monitoring and evaluation, the multi-annual budget programming and budgetary flexibility, and of public procurement in line with *acquis* requirements (European Commission 2005, 61–3).

The nature and extent of domestic change

The institutionalization of NUTS 2 regions

In the immediate period after the communist breakdown, there was an important degree of misfit between EU and Romanian types of governance. During the negotiation process, the Commission made clear that prior domestic adaptation to the EU principles was a key accession condition. An early consequence of this was the introduction of a number of territorial regional units and features of multi-level governance. The changes that took place were the result of a combination of EU external pressures for reforms and changing domestic conditions.

Domestically, the coming to power in 1996 of pro-EU parties opened the path for regional reforms. They initiated a process of reflection on how to adapt to the EU conditionality in the field of cohesion policy and introduced in 1998 a formal regional layer, represented by eight NUTS 2 regions and a series of institutions charged with regional development (Law no. 151/1998). These regions are not territorial administrative units; they are associations of four to six counties without legal personality, brought together for statistical and regional development purposes and for the management and implementation of pre-accession and structural funds. They were created on the condition that they would not put into question the existing distribution of competences between the central and the local levels of government. Consequently, they have no political or fiscal power and therefore no policy-making powers.

The following section provides an overview of other relevant changes, with a focus on those aspects relating to the vertical and horizontal dimensions of multi-level governance (see Bache 2010).

The vertical dimension of multi-level governance

From the beginning, the institutions charged with regional development at the national level were not very well defined and they have been subject to several modifications over time depending on the central governmental interests and ideas about regional development. In 1998, the National Agency for Regional Development (*Agenţia Naţională pentru Dezvoltare Regională* – ANDR) and the National Council for Regional Development (*Consiliul Naţional pentru Dezvoltare Regională* – CNDR) were set up, the latter being chaired by the Prime Minister. Subsequently, in June 2003, on the occasion of a government restructuring, one of the main institutions charged with the coordination of regional policy at the national level, the Ministry of Development and Prognosis, was dissolved and its tasks in the regional development field were taken over by other ministries. Among these were the Ministry of European Integration and the Ministry of Public Finance. In April 2007, a new institution was created to take over the management of regional development at the central level: the Ministry for Development, Public Works and Housing.

At the regional level, the new institutions created were the regional development councils (RDCs), which are composed of the presidents of the county councils and one representative of municipality, town and commune councils from each county member of the development regions. The government's deconcentrated representatives in the counties, the prefects, can participate in the RDCs' meetings but they do not have the right to vote.

> [The RDC] analyses and decides over the regional development strategy and the regional development programmes; it approves the regional development projects; it submits to the National Board for Regional Development proposals concerning the formation of the Regional Development Fund; it approves the criteria, priorities, allotment and destination of the resources of the Regional Development Fund; it checks the utilization of the funds allotted to the regional development agencies from the National Fund for Regional Development; it checks the observance of the regional objectives. (Law no. 151/1998, Article 6)

The RDCs, as representatives of local interests meeting at regional level, are therefore the institutional actors that decide on the Regional Development Fund (the financing for the functioning of the regional institutions) and that monitor the performance of the second set of new institutions, the regional development agencies (RDAs) (discussed below).

This short description of the composition and functions of the RDCs indicates that these institutions have a fuzzy, questionable status because they are a structure of aggregated local interests that are dominated by political influences. This leads to a degree of political interference in their functioning and especially in the allocation of the EU pre-accession funds:

> although there is an independent assessment committee (formed out of independent experts), important decisions about financing large investments in the counties are either the result of negotiation or imposed by county public authorities that constitute the council. (Ghinea and Moraru 2002, 9)

The other institutions created at the regional level are eight RDAs, which are non-governmental organizations. In terms of their tasks and functioning, the RDAs develop the regional development plans and implement and promote regional development projects to be financed by Phare and co-financed by the Romanian state.

The RDAs have been designed as private, independent, voluntary association bodies of non-governmental affiliation. Nevertheless, in practice, they are far from independent. The RDAs are dependent on political nominations from the local elected authorities present in the RDCs, as well as on financial resources from the central and local budgets. Specifically, they are financed by the Regional Development Funds (RDF), which are formed of allocations from the NFRD and of various voluntary contributions from local and county budgets. The status of the RDF is not very well defined in legal terms (Pascariu et al. 2002, 42); this inhibits the proper functioning of the RDAs and makes them extremely dependent on the central and local financing and goodwill.

This situation has a dual implication. On the one hand, the less endowed subnational actors (mostly rural communes and poor, under-developed towns) do not dispose of the necessary resources in order to effectively contribute to the RDF and to assure the proper performance of their RDAs. On the other hand, the main contributors to the RDF expect a certain return of their contribution and use the RDAs as a platform for attracting funding and investment for their counties – and not necessarily for the whole region (Jordan and Popescu 2002, 14).

The horizontal dimension of multi-level governance

As noted above, the civil society in Romania has not been involved in state–non-state partnerships. Despite a low level of civil society participation in Romanian public policy-making, there are a number of sub-national initiatives that have proposed models for territorial reforms.

One example is the *Pro Transylvania Civic Foundation*, which operated between 1998 and 2000. The initiator and chairman of this foundation was Sabin Gherman, a journalist from Cluj-Napoca, who criticized Romania's centralist system of government, which was endangering Transylvania's chances of modernization and economic development (Gherman 1998). In line with his declarations from 1998, Gherman created in 2000 *Partidul Ardelenilor* (the Party of Transylvanians – PA), which defended the ideas of regionalism and proposed redrafting the current Romanian Constitution in order to encompass the regional layer and its political autonomy and self-administration.

Another sub-national initiative for political regions was the *Transylvanian Memorandum* (2001), drafted by a group of Romanian and Hungarian intellectuals from Transylvania, and organized around the journal *Provincia*. They called for a public discussion on 'Romania of regions' and proposed a regional re-organization on the basis of new administrative and political structures such as regional councils or provincial parliaments in line with the European principle of subsidiarity and the concept of 'Europe of the regions' (Memorandum 2001).

These are only a few examples of civil society organized initiatives calling for a public discussion about regions and the regional re-organization on the basis of new administrative and political structures in line with the European principles and concepts. However, in terms of direct impact of these initiatives on the national decision-making process, these actors had neither a triggering nor a shaping influence on the governmental decision to introduce statistical regions. Their role has been to bring forward the issues of regionalization and regionalism and to associate these phenomena with modernization and policy reforms on the basis of the historical regional traditions of Romania (representatives of these regional initiatives, interviews 2003 and 2005).

This evolution shows the important role of the central government in controlling the process of institutional and policy reform. The succeeding central governments, as the main interlocutors of the European Commission in the process of membership negotiations, filtered the input into the policy reform and adopted a top-down driven system, which allows for a certain degree of sub-national (local, not regional) autonomy.

At the same time, the RDAs and the other institutions responsible for regional development have increased the number of actors involved in regional policy-making. Nevertheless, the regional layer was not designed to dislocate or transform Romania's traditional centre–local public administration and territorial division.

The institutional expression of sub-national governance in Romania is therefore rather complex. There is a clear distinction between the democratically elected local authorities and the recently created non-elected regional institutions. There is also another level of distinction: the new regional institutions are task-specific (Type II multi-level governance[2] bodies), whereas local authorities enjoy a wide range of competences (Type I). If the latter have gradually become important actors in the framework of political and financial decentralization, this is not the case for the regional institutions. These regions are considered to be relatively artificial. Their creation was based on a number of criteria – such as geographical vicinity and solidarity and cohesion – aiming at bringing together more and less developed counties in economic and social terms.

However, in some regions, this has created problems – especially where there is a very sharp contrast of interests between the constituting counties. In the region South Muntenia for example, counties (such as Prahova and Arges) that enjoy an industrial development and attract foreign investment in their urbanized, tourist areas, find it very difficult to develop common interests with counties (like Calarasi, Giurgiu, Teleorman) that are very poor and dominated by agriculture.

While the institutional structure designed for regional development has its limitations and does not question the administrative and territorial organization of the state (no major changes in terms of polity), there have been significant developments in terms of the partnership through the involvement of social and economic actors from the local and regional levels. The European Commission welcomed the country's efforts for the integration and application of the partnership principle, especially which reflected in the drafting of the Regional Development Plans and the Regional Operational Programme for 2007–2013. The final form of the document was coordinated by the Ministry of European Integration (the General Direction of Regional Development) in its role as Management Authority on the basis of regional programming documents elaborated by the eight RDAs (the Implementation Authorities).

The effects of the adaptation process to the EU partnership principle were evident in the involvement of non-state actors in the drafting of the Regional Operational Programme 2007–2013. Most of the partners involved in this process, which took place throughout the whole of 2005, were the (public) regional, local and urban agencies, the ministries and governmental agencies, the social and economic partners, and the organizations of civil society, NGOs (Ministry of European Integration 2006, 8).

In the same vein, the RDAs elaborated detailed lists with the existing local and regional actors involved in this process of public consultation for determining the regions' needs and potentials of development. These included the local public administration institutions, local industry, commerce and agriculture, regional chambers, public and private universities and research centres, NGOs, environment regional agencies, economic development regional agencies, county agencies for employment and education, etc. These actors meet in the framework of the so-called Regional Consortiums: organizations that are headed and coordinated by the RDAs.

In addition to demonstrating the importance of EU requirements for increasing participation in policy-making, these developments also illustrate the importance of having integrated formal supportive institutions of regionalization to provide actors with a forum for action and give them a channel to decision-making.

Tracing the causes of domestic change

The EU as an external source of change

The majority of interviewees for this research supported the idea that the EU has influenced the Romanian territorial and administrative state structure through a number of instruments such as financial support through pre-accession funds and the creation and implementation of regional policy (officials of the Ministry of European Integration, regional development agencies and local administrations, interviews 2003 and 2005). This was complemented by the strong interest of the Romanian government for strengthening the country's administrative capacity and for preparing the country for efficiently accessing and managing the financial EU support. Along the way, the Commission constantly signalled to the Romanian governments the areas where the country was lagging behind and where investments could be made for improving the processes of internal adaptation.

Thus, the Commission strongly insisted on the necessity of creating an institutional frame dealing with regional development and corresponding to the NUTS system of territorial organization (officials from the Delegation of the European Commission to Bucharest, interviews 2003). The creation of the Romanian regions for development therefore mirrors a process of internal adaptation, politically driven and financially sustained by European pre-accession funding, with the specific aim of preparing for EU membership.

Domestic sources of change

Between 1990 and 1996, Romania was characterized by an important degree of misfit both in institutional and policy terms when compared with the EU requirements in the field of regional policy. Before Romania's official request for EU membership, no territorial regional reforms were initiated due to a combination of inhibiting domestic factors in the specific historical conjuncture of Romania's transition to democracy and preparation for EU accession.

The first factor of importance was the centralist state tradition, which was maintained and reinforced after the historical critical juncture of the end of communism by a constellation of nationalist, former communist actors who held power and centralist beliefs. This leads us to the second factor, namely the obstructive presence and action of an important number of veto players with access to power and the ability to block decision-making. This constellation of governmental actors was composed of the official inheritors of the communist party structures (the National Salvation Front – FSN, transformed into the Party of Social Democracy from Romania – PDSR) and of the nationalist, extremist parties (Party of National Unity – PUNR, and the Great Romania Party – PRM). They strongly opposed any prospect of regional reforms.

Third, and closely related to the previous variables, was the existence of a predominant domestic discourse opposed to the regions' institutionalization, which was seen as a source for state dissolution and balkanization. Finally, we can refer to the weak and marginalized existence of norm agents such as the party representatives of the ethnic Hungarian minority, the Democratic Alliance of Hungarians from Romania, UDMR, who were not allowed access to decision-making.

The important turning point in the domestic post-communist evolution was the coming to power in 1996 of the pro-Western, reformist parties, reunited under an umbrella political organization, the Democratic Convention of Romania (CDR). This consisted of the right-wing party Peasants' Christian and Democratic National Party (PNTCD), the Liberal National Party (PNL), the UDMR and the centre-left Democratic Party (PD). The governmental coalition included the UDMR, one of the main proponents of regionalization formulas for sub-state reforms and state territorial re-organization. This domestic development reflected a shift of power in Romanian politics favouring democratic reforms and promoting the country's engagement in the process of negotiations and adaptation for future EU membership.

Three additional variables contribute to explaining the domestic outcome of regional reform. First, the access to government of the pro-European, reformist party coalition led to the exclusion of veto players from the national decision-making structure, confirming therefore that the fewer the number of veto players with decision-making powers opposed to regionalization, the higher the possibility for regional reforms. The elimination of the nationalist parties from the governmental coalitions after 1996 contributed to the diminution of the conflictual centre–periphery relations, eased the opening of dialogue and negotiations with the EU and allowed for regional reforms.

Second, the results of the 1998 institutional and policy reform reflected the national government's interests and ideas about the country's future benefits as an EU member. The reform was therefore an outcome of national accommodation to EU requirements for regional policy reform, based on a rational calculus of compliance in light of the future membership benefits. The majority of the interviewees, representatives of the regional institutions, national administration and representatives of the civil society and bottom-up regionalist groups stated that the EU conditionality and the rationally constructed domestic interest to become EU member were the main rationale and driving force of reforms in the regional policy field.

Third, we emphasize the gradual change in the internal discourse on the regions' institutionalization, which started to be presented less as a threat to the integrity of the state and more as a necessary technical measure on Romania's path towards EU accession. The political governmental elites (especially the coalition in power between 1996 and 2000 and the government between 2000 and 2004) reformulated the perception on the regions' institutionalization by dissociating it, on the one hand, from any ethnical demands and, on the other hand, by presenting it as a technicality, a necessary condition for EU membership and domestic economic development.

Conclusion

Through engaging with the EU's cohesion policy and related pre-accession instruments, the Romanian polity has become more compound and exhibits features of multi-level governance. Despite this, central government ministries remain dominant.

The process of regional governance reform in Romania has led to structural changes at the regional level, but these adjustments reflect more an overall national pre-occupation with responding to the Commission's requirements and preferences rather than any domestic attachment to any type of regionalized state organization. However, although the limits of regionalization are perceptible in Romania, changes in response to EU conditionality have also led to the emergence of new patterns of governance based on partnership and subsidiarity and the re-introduction in the domestic political vocabulary of concepts such as political regionalization.

The EU's normative and material conditionality is considered in light of the empirical evidence as a necessary condition for change towards multi-level governance. The timing of the territorial reforms has been clearly influenced by EU pressures for internal change, particularly in the accession period. Given that post-communist Romania had no regional institutional structures and has been constitutionally defined as a centralized, unitary state, the internal institutionalization of regions and the creation of regional development policy provide an example of how EU conditionality triggers domestic change and adaptation. The introduction in Romania of the NUTS 2 type of regions is an adaptational response of the national governmental actors to the EU pressures for establishing statistical regions in order to assure a successful EU membership and subsequent regional funding.

On the one hand, EU conditionality focused on very practical matters of funds management, administrative and territorial organization on the basis of NUTS division, partnership at the level of policy design and implementation absorption capacity, and regional administrative capacity. These elements are far from implying the necessity of introducing regional governments or reforming the state territorial organization and the division of competences between the traditional administrative and territorial layers (central and local). The Commission's recommendations and conditionality clearly insisted on more managerial and administrative issues (Keating 2003) rather than on polity changes that would open the way for a widespread process of political regionalization and governance reform.

On the other hand, another level of EU impact, apart from the institutional one, is related to the emergence of new opportunities for regional and local actors. New regional and local private actors emerged such as regional and county associations which opened representations in Brussels. Groups of citizens, mainly university professors and journalists, started writing manifestos on regionalization and new regional political parties were created. Accordingly, the EU's impact led to the emergence of new patterns of governance involving the recognition of regional state and non-state actors as valid and necessary partners in the drafting and implementation of regional and cohesion policy.

While EU conditionality is important here, it is not a sufficient condition for change. Our analysis shows that only the combination of external and domestic conditions has caused the regional reforms in Romania. In summary, these causal conditions are: (1) the material and normative EU conditionality; (2) the blocked access of veto players to the national decision-making system; (3) the interest of national governmental elites to assure a successful EU accession and access to structural funds; and (4) the prevailing presence of a domestic discourse associating the regions' institutionalization with economic development and successful EU accession.

In terms of reform outcomes, it can be argued that EU cohesion policy in Romania has had a more significant impact on Type II multi-level governance than Type I. It has spawned new agencies (notably the regional development agencies) and other bodies set up with a specific functional remit. These developments and Romania's response to the partnership principle has had a pluralizing effect on the polity.

In terms of Type I multi-level governance, the Romanian Constitution does not recognize the newly created regions as state administrative units. According to the constitution, only counties, municipalities and villages are territorial administrative units, which are considered legal entities of public law, benefiting from property rights and full legal capacity. The democratically accountable institutions are located at the local/county and central state levels. These regions did not directly undermine existing institutions and the existing distribution of competences between the central and the local levels of government. They lack the democratic accountability provided by direct popular elections and they have not yet succeeded in mobilizing and aggregating regional interests.

At the same time, a nuance must be brought forward. Even though the core of domestic institutions and the distribution of competences between the territorial layers remain relatively unchanged, regional institutions have moved forward slowly and hesitatingly, building their performance and social legitimacy on the EU framework of regional policy and structural funds. Most recently, and primarily through consultation, they are gradually becoming integrated into the framework of regional development policy, thus increasing the role assigned to them when created in 1998. In short, the developments to date in relation to multi-level governance are significant but may prove to be more so as time goes by.

Notes

1. The analysis is based on several sources of data including academic literature, secondary documents (newspapers), primary material (historical data) and interviews. The interviews were conducted at the last phase of a fieldwork process, which included the following stages. First, a documentary search took place (i.e. all relevant key documents on cohesion policy were consulted). Subsequently, a list of key organizations relevant to the area of cohesion policy was identified. Next, I contacted and interviewed 28 elite level actors. When selecting the interviewees, the aim was to get a good representation from (1) national government officials/politicians (eight representatives from several central ministries charged with regional development, among which the Ministry of European Integration, Directorate for Regional Politics and Development); (2) sub-national government officials/politicians (three directors of the Agencies for Regional Development, eight representatives of local administration at the level of county councils represented in the regional development councils); (3) EU officials (two representatives of the Commission Delegation to Bucharest); (4) civil society actors; (5) other influential and/or informed actors (eight representatives of civil society and initiators of bottom-up regionalist initiatives).
2. Here, I draw on the two types of multi-level governance developed by Marks and Hooghe (2004; see also Bache 2010). Type I multi-level governance describes system-wide governing arrangements in which the dispersion of authority is restricted to a limited number of clearly defined, non-overlapping jurisdictions at a limited number of territorial levels, each of which has responsibility for a 'bundle' of functions. By contrast, Type II multi-level governance describes governing arrangements in which the jurisdiction of authority is task-specific, where jurisdictions operate at numerous territorial levels and may be overlapping.

References

Bache, I. 2010. Europeanization and multi-level governance: EU cohesion policy and pre-accession aid in Southeast Europe. *Southeast European and Black Sea Studies* 10, no. 1: 1–12.

Bădescu, G. 2008. Democratizare, valori şi educaţie şcolară [Democratization, values and school education]. In *Barometrul de Opinie Publică 1998–2007*, 78–90. Bucharest: Soros Foundation Romania.

Dobre, A.M. Forthcoming. Romania: From historical regions to local decentralization via the unitary state. In *The handbook of sub-national democracy in the European Union*, ed. J. Loughlin, F. Hendriks, and A. Lidstrom. Oxford: Oxford University Press.

European Commission. 1997. *Agenda 2000 – Commission opinion about Romania*. Brussels: Office for Official Publications of the European Communities.

European Commission. 2002. *Communication from the Commission to the Council and the European Parliament: Roadmaps for Bulgaria and Romania, Brussels* (November 13). Brussels: Office for Official Publications of the European Communities.

European Commission. 2005. *Romania 2005 comprehensive monitoring report*. Brussels: Office for Official Publications of the European Communities.

European Commission. 2006. *Romania May 2006 monitoring report*. Brussels: Office for Official Publications of the European Communities.

Gherman, S. 1998. *M-amsăturat de România* [I am fed up with Romania]. Cluj-Napoca: Monitorul de Cluj (September 16).

Ghinea, A., and A. Moraru. 2002. *Aspects regarding the decentralization process in Romania: The administrative-territorial reform.* Institute for Public Policies. Bucharest: Open Society Foundation.

Hitchins, K. 1996. *The Romanians, 1774–1866.* Oxford: Oxford University Press.

Jordan, P., and C. Popescu. 2002. *The Europe of the regions: Strategies and perspectives in the view of the forthcoming enlargement of the European Union (Part II on Bulgaria, Latvia, Lithuania, Malta, Romania, Slovakia and Turkey). Study on behalf of the Committee of the Regions of the European Union.* Brussels: Committee of the Regions.

Keating, M. 2003. Regionalisation in Central and Eastern Europe: The diffusion of a western model? In *The regional challenge in Central and Eastern Europe: Territorial restructuring and European integration*, ed. M. Keating and J. Hughes, 51–67. Brussels: Peter Lang.

Local Government and Public Service Reform Initiative. 2009. *Romania overview on local government.* http://lgi.osi.hu/country_datasheet.php.

Marks, G., and L. Hooghe. 2004. Contrasting visions of multi-level governance. In *Multi-level governance*, ed. I. Bache and M. Flinders, 15–30. Oxford: Oxford University Press.

Matei, G., P. Antonevici, A. Popa, and V. Giosan. 2003. Romania. In *Sub-national data requirements for fiscal decentralization: Case studies from Central and Eastern Europe*, ed. S. Yilmaz, J. Hegedus, and M. Bell, 59–86. Washington, DC: World Bank.

Memorandum. 2001. Memorandum to parliament on Romania's regional construction. *Ziua*, December 12. English version: BBC Monitoring Service, UK, December 12.

Ministry of European Integration. 2006. *The regional operational programme for 2007–2013, Bucharest*, March. Bucharest: Ministry of European Integration.

Morar, F. 2002. The way out and the way in: Post-communism and democracy in Romania. *Romanian Political Science Review* 2, no. 1: 77–113.

Papadimitriou, D., and D. Phinnemore. 2004. Europeanization, conditionality and domestic change: The twinning exercise and administrative reform in Romania. *Journal of Common Market Studies* 42, no. 3: 619–39.

Pascariu, G., M. Stanculescu, D. Jula, and M. Lutas. 2002. *Impactul Politicii de Coeziune Sociala asupra Dezvoltarii Economico-Sociale la Nivel Regional in România.* Pre-accession Impact Study of the European Institute from Romania 9. Bucharest: Romanian European Institute.

Europeanization and nascent multi-level governance in Croatia

Ian Bache[a] and Danijel Tomšić[b]

[a]Department of Politics, University of Sheffield, Sheffield, UK; [b]South East European Centre, City College Thessaloniki, University of Sheffield, Sheffield, UK

This contribution considers whether the EU's pre-accession instruments of cohesion policy are contributing to the development of a more compound polity in Croatia and, specifically, considers the extent to which there is a process of Europeanization characterized by emergent features of multi-level governance. It argues that while some features of multi-level governance are emerging in Croatia, the emphasis of EU programmes is at this stage on national implementation and central government has to date proved adept at shaping and steering the partnerships and networks induced at national level. Sub-nationally, there is greater activity independent of central government, and some evidence of a deeper learning taking place, with EU-inspired activities and practices being transferred to other spheres.

Introduction

This contribution analyses the effects of EU pre-accession aid relating to cohesion policy on governance in Croatia. The next section provides a brief background on the nature of governance and politics in Croatia. The third gives an overview of the relevant EU policy instruments operating in Croatia, past and present. The fourth section includes the main findings from the interviews and other research undertaken for this study.[1] It highlights the main developments that have taken place in relation to multi-level governance before considering the vertical and horizontal dimensions, respectively.[2] The fifth examines the causes of domestic change and the 'Conclusion' section argues that the implementation system for pre-accession aid is centralized and national government retains control over the key domestic policy-making processes. However, against the backbone of central dominance, some nascent features of multi-level governance have emerged that may not be easy to roll back while EU membership remains on the agenda.

Governance and politics in Croatia

According to Schmidt's (2006) typologies, Croatia can broadly be defined as a simple polity, being a state with a combination of a majoritarian system of representation, statist policy-making processes and a unitary state structure. In former Yugoslavia, no intermediary authorities existed between the federal republics and the local units of self-government. Until 1993, when counties where established, Croatia lacked an intermediate tier of government and public services were highly centralized and politicized. Unitarism still enjoys a high level of political support, not least because Croatia fought a war in order to secure its sovereignty and territorial integrity over separatist movements in the early 1990s. The constitution of 1990 centralized power and established a semi-presidential system, which was modelled after the Constitution of the V French Republic and tailored to Franjo Tudjman (Zakosek 2004, 684) and stipulated a 'unitary and inseparable' Croatian state.

After the early years of nation-building, some issues of decentralization began to interest the epistemic community and local actors (Kopric 2004, 3–4). However, engaging in regional policy was seen in some quarters as fraught with danger: political initiatives in the Istrian region very soon tried to ensure a larger degree of regional independence and, therefore, generated great opposition from the centre (Institute for International Relations [IMO], senior researcher, interview 2008). However, after Tudjman's death and the change of government to centre-left in 2000, broad revisions of the constitution not only changed the political system from semi-presidential to parliamentary, but also marked the beginning of a decentralization process by defining counties as intermediary units of self-governance (Kopric 2004, 5–6). This decentralization was given a legal basis with the adoption of the Law on Local and Regional Self-Government in April 2001 (Zakosek 2004, 720).

There are currently 21 counties in Croatia, one of them being the city of Zagreb. The county level manages affairs pertaining to education, health care, physical and urban planning, economic development, transport and transport infrastructure (Sumpor 2007, 10–11). The counties do not have their own financial resources, but are dependent financially on the centre (Zakosek 2004, 721). The decentralization of public administration is one of the major goals of Croatian public administration reform. Kopric (2004, 19–20) argued for a strengthening of the legal position of local self-government, enhanced financial resources and financial autonomy, an expansion of administrative tasks and a deepening of democratic legitimacy. Some of these processes are under way, most notably with personal elections at the local and regional level being held for the first time in 2009; previously, elections took place between parties and the winning party would decide the individuals elected post-election.

In relation to policy-making processes, Croatia has a tradition of tripartism that allows for the involvement of employers' associations and trade unions in policy-making processes and public debates. These organizations often formally act in advisory bodies to the government, such as the National Competitiveness Council, or on ad hoc issues when experts are required. Beyond this, the participation of civil society actors in Croatian public policy-making has been weak. They have traditionally lacked the relevant resources to participate effectively and have been given little or no encouragement by government to do so.

In sum, governance and politics in Croatia is in sharp contrast to the complex compound polity that is the EU (Schmidt 2006; see Bache 2010) and that is reflected in the requirements for cohesion policy and – to a lesser extent – for pre-accession aid. Therefore, we can expect some degree of misfit with established arrangements in Croatia that will require significant adjustment.

The relevant pre-accession instruments

Croatia's domestic regional policy post-communism has been limited in its scope and coverage, generally focusing on assisting the regions most affected by the 'homeland war'. While policies have since extended to the islands and hilly areas, there is no comprehensive domestic regional policy in Croatia to date, although steps are being taken in that direction (below).

The EU pre-accession instruments available to Croatia have changed over time, due both to closer relations with the EU and to systemic changes in EU funding. From 1996 until 2000, Croatia had the Obnova (Reconstruction) programme of technical assistance and subsequently the Community Assistance for Reconstruction, Development and Stabilisation (CARDS), which Croatia used between 2001 and 2004. CARDS was aimed at strengthening Croatia's participation in the Stabilization and Association Process with particular reference to: the strengthening of integrated border control; support for democratic stabilization and increasing the capacity of state institutions; and regional infrastructure and environment protection.

After receiving the status of a candidate country in 2004, Croatia became eligible for the pre-accession programmes Phare, ISPA and Sapard (CODEF [Central Office for Development Strategy and Coordination of EU Funds] 2007, 9). These programmes were replaced by the Instrument for Pre-Accession Assistance (IPA) for the period 2007–2013. The IPA incorporates five components: (1) transition assistance and institution building; (2) cross-border cooperation; (3) regional development; (4) human resources development; and (5) rural development. The funds allocated to Croatia under the five IPA components amounted to €749.83 million in the period between 2007 and 2011, the largest amount of €257.35 million being earmarked for the regional development component.

The nature and extent of domestic change

Key developments

As noted above, the misfit between EU and Croatian modes of governance is high and so is the degree of adaptational pressure. In relation to the pre-accession instruments for cohesion policy, the available funds generate sufficient 'external incentives' for states to develop institutional and policy models that will meet European requirements (Jacoby 2005, 94). In this case, it has been made clear by the Commission that only by harmonizing legislation and institutions with European principles prior to accession, would Croatia be able to fully access the available funds from the beginning of EU membership. The consequence has been significant domestic changes in Croatia. We begin here by giving an overview of the Croatian response to the requirements, with a particular focus on those aspects relating most closely to Type I and Type II multi-level governance.[3]

The concept of regional operational programmes (ROPs) was introduced in Croatia under the EU CARDS programme in 2001. Although described as 'regional', in this case the term refers to county level. Initially, ROPs were prepared in six counties with the technical assistance of the United Nations Development Programme (UNDP). Subsequently, ROPs were prepared for all the other counties except Zagreb. They were originally designed to encompass both international (EU and other donors) and domestic sources of funding. Up to this point, the focus of all domestic development policy was on the reconstruction of a small number of war-torn areas. However, while ROPs were introduced, they were not implemented: at the time of writing, the government law and strategy that would give them the administrative capacity and funding to be implemented had not been agreed (below).

In 2002, the Croatian government established its own Fund for Regional Development (FRD), which became operational in 2003 with the objective of providing assistance to counties and local units. It funds development projects (acceptable to government criteria) in counties and local units with a GDP per capita of less than 65% of the national average. The Fund originally had a staff of five people, but this had grown to 12 by 2008.

In 2006, the government created CODEF to create a distinct area of competence for the EU funds. CODEF would provide continuity in the handling of EU funds within Croatia and was a signal that the government understood the importance of effective organization for the EU funding. CODEF was established as a government agency independent of any government department and answerable directly to the Prime Minister's Office. It was made the leading institution in the accession negotiations on regional policy and the coordination of structural instruments.

In response to the Commission prompting, Croatia embarked on a series of measures in preparation for managing and implementing the structural funds post-accession. Several programming documents were introduced, of which the Strategic Development Framework adopted in 2006 (and covering the period 2007–2013) was the most important.[4] The main goal of this framework is 'to ensure development in a competitive market economy acting within a modern welfare state' (CODEF 2006, 4).

It identifies 10 strategic areas for the realization of this goal. Two of those areas, namely transport and energy – as well as environment and regional development – link directly to the EU pre-accession funds. The strategy highlights the need for establishing a harmonized system for joint action and partnership between central-, regional- and local-level institutions and the necessity of a regional development act. It further foresees the establishment of development agencies to stimulate and support development activities in the counties, to promote county partnerships for development, and to build up the already existing entrepreneurial infrastructure (CODEF 2006, 44).

In the attempt to organize the absorption of structural funds, the Strategic Coherence Framework 2007–2013 was finalized in 2007, coordinated by the CODEF. This framework is a key programming document that serves as a reference point for the use of the EU assistance available for Croatia through IPA Component 3 (regional development) and Component 4 (human resource development), which will later translate into the structural funds. As such, those components are expected to follow the partnership and programming principles of the structural funds, which are particularly relevant for research on multi-level governance (see Bache 2010). However, the administration of IPA in Croatia would be national rather than at county level.

In its 2008 progress report on Croatia's accession process, the European Commission noted that Croatia:

> still needs to pursue its efforts in order to meet the regulatory requirements for cohesion policy, mainly by amending the Budget Act to ensure full multi-annual budget programming and budget flexibility and by adopting the Regional Development Act that will provide a broad legal framework for implementation of the regional policy. (European Commission 2008, 50)

While three NUTS 2 regions[5] had been agreed in March 2007 for administrative purposes (Northwestern Croatia, six counties; Eastern Croatia, eight counties; and

Adriatic Croatia, seven counties) at the the time of writing (mid-2009) the regional infrastructure at NUTS 2 level required by the Commission for managing the structural funds and Cohesion Fund post-accession had not been developed. Interviewees suggested that: 'probably one part will in the beginning be centrally distributed, either through the CODEF or another institution, until those institutions enable themselves and equip themselves with people and fund' (Chamber of Commerce official, interview 2008).

At the national level, the Ministry of Regional Development, Forestry and Water Management (MRD), which was created in 2008, had been appointed the coordinating body for regional development issues, and a department for Integrated Regional Development had been formed within the predeceasing Ministry. At the local and regional level, administrative units responsible for EU integration and regional development had also been established. In addition, the overwhelming majority of counties and cities had established county or local development agencies, entrepreneurship centres, technology centres and other development institutions, which dealt with economic and other development issues at the regional and local level.

At this time, the responsible cabinet minister informed the public that the regional development strategy would be sent into parliamentary procedure before the summer break of 2009, emphasizing its importance for the absorption of cohesion funds post-accession. However, it remained unclear how regional policy would be implemented legally and who in practice would be in charge for the management, planning and implementation of funds. As one interviewee put it: 'The regional development agencies were founded on the basis of a draft law on regional development, and now three years later, it is not yet implemented' (regional development agency for the Varazdin County Development Agency [AZRA] official, interview 2008).

The vertical dimension of multi-level governance

The central government ministries were undoubtedly the key players in the domestic networks related to EU funds. CODEF, as the coordinating institution and the lead body on accession negotiations over regional and structural policies, was pivotal. However, depending on the particular policy area or funding stream, different central departments would be more important. For example, the Ministry of Sea, Transport and Infrastructure (MSTI), the Ministry of Environment and Physical Planning and Construction (MEPC) and the Ministry of Economy, Labour and Entrepreneurship (MELE), each prepared the operational plans for their fields of engagement (Institute of Economics Zagreb [EIZ] researcher, interview 2008).

In addition, the MRD has responsibility for the regional development strategy, the Central State Office for Administration (CSOA) for training, and the Ministry of Finance for budget allocation and various financial exercises related to EU funds (Chamber of Commerce official, interview 2008).

As a government agency responsible for coordination, CODEF occupied a unique position within this network. While it had a degree of autonomy from department control, which gave it greater flexibility to act in response to EU demands, it was also a politically weak agency. Unlike the line ministries mentioned, it was not headed by a cabinet minister (but by a non-cabinet state secretary) and thus carried less formal weight in government. So while it was in many respects central to the network, it could also be omitted from strategic decisions if other ministries deemed this appropriate. As such, it is an important illustration of acknowledging the complexity at the heart of government in relation to the coordination and control over the planning and implementation of EU programmes.

Interviews and documents revealed fairly widespread participation in the development of strategy and planning documents as well as extensive engagement through conferences and seminars. However, despite moves in the direction of greater consultation with sub-national actors, the response of sub-national interviewees to developments remained generally critical of government action on this, but very positive towards EU programmes and actors. Interviewees suggested that there was a distinction between national attempts at regional policy, which aimed at advancing 'pet projects' of central ministries, while EU funding was awarded more on the basis of the quality of project proposals.

Moreover, sub-national actors from county authorities and county development agencies often felt that their participation in policy-making was tolerated rather than welcomed and that their input was largely ignored. As one county official put it:

> In certain phases they consult us and ask for our opinion, but ideas or criticism which I have given, I have not found in the final drafts. The national level has no obligation to incorporate this into a legal solution … We as [county] institutions have no influence that our word has to be heard. That is the structure. (Interview 2008)

However, there was also acknowledgement that central ministries had 'opened up' a little to sub-national actors because of EU pressures (Istrian Development Agency [IDA] official, interview 2008).

Generally, sub-national actors felt they had little influence on creating the overarching development strategies and the transition to IPA. In this sense, there was no significant redistribution of influence between centre and sub-national units and thus the effect to date of EU programmes on the vertical dimension of multi-level governance had been low. Overall, counties and local institutions lacked the capacity to participate effectively in many areas of policy-making. However, it was felt that those counties most well-connected to the centre politically had more impact on policy-making, as well as better access to funding (UNDP official, interview 2008).

However, while not improving their position significantly vis-à-vis central government through the opportunities created by EU pre-accession aid, there were other effects on the sub-national level that may have longer-term implications. In particular, there was much greater interaction between Croatian sub-national authorities as a result of EU engagement. While some counties sought to create development agencies in-house, others created development agencies jointly with other counties or other sub-national units. Sometimes, these development agencies were co-owned by other sub-national government units. Alongside development agencies have emerged an array of other local bodies and activities, such as centres for entrepreneurship, technology parks and enterprise zones, each of which has engaged various local (state and non-state) actors in their development and operation. The overall impact is a much more differentiated pattern of activity at sub-national level, with features of Type II multi-level governance.

These developments can be attributed primarily, but not exclusively, to EU effects. EU technical assistance has been crucial to the establishment of county development agencies and other bodies and organizations mentioned above. Moreover, personnel from local authorities, NGOs and other local organizations have received EU-funded training on issues such as project development, project management and public–private partnerships. However, other international agencies and organizations (World

Bank, USAID and UNDP) have provided financial support for local authorities (Fund for Regional Development of the Republic of Croatia [FRR] official, interview 2008). For example, the World Bank supported the *Croatia Social and Economic Recovery Project*, which aids institutional development at central and local level (civil society organizations and local self-government), in planning, monitoring and maintaining projects.

The horizontal dimension of multi-level governance

As noted in the introduction, with the exception of the role played by the social partners in tripartite arrangements over discreet areas of policy, civil society in Croatia has traditionally been very weak. As such, the prospects for strongly interdependent state – non-state partnerships developing in the pre-accession period was strictly limited. However, there was no doubt that engagement between state and non-state actors had increased significantly through EU initiatives and pressures and that non-state actors had participated in policy-making at several points.

To date, the most prominent contributions have been made by the IMO and the EIZ, which have participated in the accession negotiations working groups of Chapter 22 (on *regional policy and coordination of structural instruments*). More specifically, the IMO helped with screening the policy field and worked on fields critical to the further development of cohesion policy (IMO senior researcher, interview 2008) and the EIZ collaborates with the former Ministry of Public Works and Reconstruction, subsequently the MRD (and specifically with its department for Integrated Regional Development). Cooperation began on a *Gesellschaft für Technische Zusammenarbeit* project on regional development planning and capacity building in 2001. In 2002 and 2003, EIZ continued its engagement in a CARDS project on capacity building and EIZ was subsequently part of the ex-ante evaluation team for the first draft of the National Strategy for Regional Development (EIZ research associate, interview 2008). In addition, the Centre for SME and Entrepreneurship Policy (CEPOR) was involved in the analysis of various aspects of SME policy at the invitation of the MELE.

As noted above, in some areas of policy the social partners have been regularly engaged by government and have influenced decision-making. This has extended to aspects of the EU accession process. The Chamber of Commerce has been involved in the whole negotiation process, with around 40 of its employees being involved in various accession negotiation working groups. However, questions relating to the working domains of ministries dominated negotiation meetings with the Commission, which left only very limited opportunities for other organizations to participate. One negotiator stated:

> I have thought that there would be a higher chance for the impact of academia in the negotiations and as the negotiator I tried to include people from scientific institutions in the negotiations working group, which I also did. However, in these negotiations in the end everything related to public administration. People from the ministries had the main word, who had to say how much their ministries and their regulations were in line with the acquis. Academia listened to that, but there was no influence. The entry into the EU actually foremost means the alignment of the national institutional apparatus with procedures and institutions. (Chamber of Commerce official, interview 2008)

The Ministry of Foreign Affairs and European Integration (MFAEI) held an informal, but nonetheless important position in the policy network for two reasons. First, as the ministry responsible for the EU accession negotiations overall it has the advantage of both participating in a wide range of meetings and coordinating a range of activities related to regional and structural policies. Moreover, it provided the link to the EU institutions for other ministries, and especially to the relevant DGs in the European Commission through its EU mission in Brussels (MFAEI official, interview 2008). Second, there was an extensive rotation of staff between its preceding institution, the Ministry of European Integration, and CODEF, which meant there were good informal links between MFAEI and CODEF that were important for day-to-day coordination.

In relation to opportunities for engagement beyond the accession negotiations, the preparation of the Strategic Development Framework provided a good example of wide participation. This document was prepared by CODEF, with input from the relevant line ministries, the EIZ and the National Competitiveness Council. The process was open to the input of economic and social partners at various stages, including the Croatian Employers' Association, the Croatian Chamber of Economy, the Association of Small and Medium Enterprises, trade unions, the Economic and Social Council and civil society associations (CODEF 2006, 7). A similar engagement of a wide range of actors occurred in the preparation of the Strategic Coherence Framework. While CODEF was the leading institution, the line ministries were again included in the preparation of the document. The development of both the Strategic Coherence Framework and of operational programmes was supported by CARDS funding.

However, while participation in these processes was widespread, influence was not. Interviewees suggested that in areas of agenda setting and development of strategies there was less genuine partnership activity than at the implementation stage. Policy goals were generally set by the ministries:

> They work by identifying where the goals are in conflict rather than identifying common goals ... Either in policy development or legislature development you would have a paper prepared that is then circulated around the relevant ministries, they give their opinions on it and as I say, if there is nothing in there which conflicts with whatever they do, its OK. (CEPOR official, interview 2008)

Moreover, foreign consultants were generally engaged to help central government with the development of strategic documents. While this may have brought short-term benefits in terms of completing the documents, this also curtailed the development of the relevant capabilities within domestic actors. The net effect of the way in which strategic documents were developed was that, despite the wide consultation, there was little sense of collective ownership of the strategies that emerged (CODEF official II, interview 2008).

Tracing the causes of domestic change

There was unanimity among interviewees that the accession process was the overwhelming factor in shaping governance change in Croatia. This was both in relation to direct effects of the *acquis*, but also in framing debate on change: the membership incentive was very influential in changing both the discourse and practice of domestic actors. At the domestic level, central government ministries have been instrumental in developing new structures and processes of governance and also in facilitating and/or denying access for other actors to participate in these.

International organizations such as the UNDP and USAID have, as discussed above, played an important role in limited spheres of activity – particularly in the early post-war period before extensive EU involvement and particularly in the war-affected areas. In addition, the World Bank has influenced the development of certain sectoral policies where it has been directly engaged with relevant ministries. Overall, though the impact of the EU on governance change in Croatia has been wider and deeper than that of other international organizations.

As illustrated above, Croatia has produced and implemented a wide range of policy instruments in response to EU requirements. Here, the combination of powerful financial incentives and the enthusiasm to complete accession led to a transformation in domestic policies and practices in the field of regional development. The national-level response has tended to be strategic, with partnerships established primarily to satisfy EU requirements or to advance central government objectives. Similarly, the creation of agencies such as CODEF and the Contracting and Financing Agency (to oversee funding issues) was driven by a rationalist logic: central government delegated complex tasks, for which it had no effective in-house capacity, while maintaining a firm grip on the meta-governance of these delegated governance arrangements. Yet while the learning process evident here is generally 'thin' rather than 'thick', there is significant manifestation of Type II multi-level governance effects through pre-accession aid in Croatia. Moreover, at the sub-national level, there is evidence of some shifts in preferences through EU activity.

The sub-national level

Sub-national institutions remain weak within Croatian governance and politics. Interviewees emphasized the ongoing financial weaknesses of the counties as a key problem and the issue of fiscal decentralization was hotly contested. The consequence is that counties – particularly in regions lagging behind – often lacked the human resources to participate in consultation processes. They also had very limited capacity for either preparing project proposals or implementing projects given and had a weak understanding of the processes involved in effective regional development policy. Some politically stronger counties had the potential to exert influence, but this was not welcomed by the Commission, which saw the potential for this to lead to clientielism and to endanger the coherence of the whole process. Thus, the domestic processes were generally dominated by national actors. As one county official (interview 2008) put it: 'in the end the Ministry for Regional Development is most important for leading regional policy. It practically drafts the regional development strategy, and prepares the law'.

In this respect, the situation in Croatia is not uncommon. In the 2004 accession process, former communist states tended to have weak sub-national capacity (see Hughes, Sasse, and Gordon 2002). In the first phase of this process, the Commission saw an opportunity to promote the sub-national level and, in some cases, regionalization, only to change its position as accession drew closely. The lack of capacity at sub-national level was such that, so as to not jeopardize the accession process, the Commission switched its focus to developing effective central capacity to ensure the funds were administered in time (Marcou 2002, 25). Under IPA, there are only national programmes in Croatia and, Commission officials informed us, in the first wave of accession the operational programmes would remain national (the guiding principle being that of 'simplicity').

However, in the Croatian case, there is evidence that the sub-national cooperation promoted by the EU has begun to have wider implications. The partnership require-ment and other activities related to EU funding brought together sub-national actors from different localities that had not previously been brought together by other means. This increased levels of communication and promoted an awareness of shared goals. Based on the increasing knowledge about the importance of programming, regional and local players have begun to exchange information through various networks. This activity has been further stimulated by the creation of NUTS 2 regions and the antic-ipated development of related administrative capacity for strategic development, which will require further inter-county cooperation.

More generally, there has been a rapid growth in sub-national activity in recent years, based largely around the counties. For example, AZRA, the regional develop-ment agency for the Varazdin County, brought together some 50 members, all being regional and local development organizations, in a *Regional Development Initiative*. This initiative provides a platform for the exchange of information and best practices among regional and local partners across Croatia. AZRA also initiated the establish-ment of the Croatian Regions office in Brussels, in which nine other counties take part. The office serves as a two-way conduit for Croatian counties, seeking to lobby the EU institutions for various forms of support, but also to keep its member institu-tions abreast of relevant developments. In addition, part of its mission is to build links with sub-national actors and their networks elsewhere in the EU (AZRA official, interview 2008).

A further example of growing sub-national activity is the initiative of the IDA and the Istria county to create a network of development agencies connected to the Adriatic Sea. All counties that are part of the Adriatic NUTS 2 region are members of this initiative. Its main aim is to prepare the counties for collaborating in programming and the preparation and implementation of projects under the NUTS 2 umbrella. A first international conference on *Regional Development of the Adriatic Euroregion and Southeastern Europe* took place in 2007, attracting a range of foreign partners from neighbouring countries. At the time of writing, counties in the other NUTS 2 regions were contemplating a similar initiative. Already, it has become a common-place for regional development agencies to communicate with each other and explore areas of common interest. Some have institutionalized regular monthly meetings to discuss the content of ROPs and development strategies and to see what activity might be best addressed above individual county level.

In short, actor behaviour and preferences at the sub-national level have shown considerable change over the past few years and, directly or otherwise, EU activity generally and pre-accession aid specifically has provided impetus for this.

Conclusion

Europeanization is an omnipresent phenomenon in Croatia, the accession process setting the agenda in a wide range of policy fields. The EU requirements have been instrumental in fostering change in the structures, processes and – to some extent – beliefs in public administration. At the central level, government actors have accepted that the price of membership is the transfer of some decisional competences to the EU and also changes to policies and processes in the domestic arena. Quite naturally, central government has sought to meet EU conditions, but at minimal cost to its domestic policy control. Thus, it has consulted, created partnerships and developed networks in line with the requirements of EU pre-accession aid, but has generally sought to control partnerships, steer networks and take from consultation processes selectively and strategically. In addition, it has created task-specific agencies, but with the explicit intention of reaching its own policy goals more effectively.

Thus, in Croatia, there is much increased activity and participation in the networks surrounding central government and many of the developments – agencies, partnerships, working groups – are characteristic of Type II multi-level governance. To date though, the Croatian government has proved an effective gatekeeper over the main channels of influence both externally (with the EU) and internally and has shaped the ground rules for the new governance arrangements that have emerged.

At the sub-national level, there is more activity autonomous of central government, although this should not be taken to mean that it is in conflict with central government objectives. Sub-national activity has been stimulated by a range of policies and initiatives emanating from the EU, other international organizations, and central government itself. However, of these, the EU has emerged as most important. Our research revealed widespread sub-national support for the policies and processes of EU pre-accession aid and for the Commission, which was widely perceived as an ally. Again, there is nothing unfamiliar in this story: EU pre-accession aid (and particularly from IPA) provides sub-national actors with important resources: financial, most obviously as end recipients of assistance, but also resources of political legitimacy through giving them a formal role in the policy process through the requirements of partnership and programming in particular. Similarly, that sub-national actors are not yet fully able to take advantage of the opportunities offered is a familiar story in the history of the accession of other heavily centralized states.

At this stage, the financial resources available through IPA Components 3 and 4 are relatively limited, as are the opportunities for sub-national actors to significantly influence policies: partnership is often more about consultation and even information-giving than collaborative policy-making. However, there is a belief at the sub-national level of there being real and lasting opportunities provided by the EU and a desire to be well placed to take advantage of such opportunities in the longer term. There is a level of dynamism evident in some of the newer bodies created through these activities at both national and sub-national level that is in contrast with the longer-established ministries of central government. Indeed, interviewees reported a contrast between the dynamism of some of the newer central agencies and the more staid approach of long-established departments. It is in the dynamism of these new bodies that the potential for significant and lasting change is most obvious. They are not bound by historical institutional legacies, but have a fresh start and are often contain a high proportion of younger staff, often trained or educated abroad, with a wider perspective than most civil servants.

Of course, as with all of the developments discussed above, the importance of dynamic new institutions will only be known in the longer term. These developments are still at a very early stage and there is nothing inevitable about the current trajectory, which points to a growing importance of the sub-national level and perhaps even a more participatory political culture. While some of these developments chime with domestic priorities or are viewed as a reasonable price for EU membership, there remain pockets of resistance to the degree and pace of change that link to entrenched interests in central government.

Moreover – and here is the importance of time and timing in the explanation – the history of previous enlargements shows that the initial burst of enthusiasm for and compliance with EU requirements is not always sustained post-accession. At the moment, conditions are relatively conducive for change: the EU's pre-accession aid policy reached a point in its evolution in 2007 when the requirements of partnership and programming became prominent, against a backdrop in which member states were increasingly uncomfortable with the prospect of further enlargement, thus raising the bar for Croatian compliance even higher.

The consequence has been small changes in the direction of multi-level governance that have made the Croatian polity somewhat more compound. To what extent these changes are consolidated and become embedded in domestic practices, we wait to see, but it is difficult to envisage these early-stage developments being entirely rolled back while the prospect of EU membership remains realistic. Ironically perhaps, the more the accession process is prolonged, the more the expectations of sub-national and non-state actors will have adjusted to the EU norms, making a domestic reversal of nascent multi-level governance even more difficult post-accession.

Acknowledgements

This study draws on research funded by the UK Economic and Social Research Council (Multi-level Governance in Southeast Europe, ESRC grant no. RES-062-23-0183). We would like to thank the ESRC for its support and the two anonymous referees for the journal for their helpful comments on earlier versions of this article. All the usual disclaimers apply.

Notes

1. In the period between January and September 2008, 18 semi-structured expert-interviews were conducted with representatives of the following organizations: FRR; CODEF (1) Department for European Union Programmes for Strengthening Institutional Capacity for Accession, (2) Department for European Union Programmes for Promoting Economic and Social Cohesion; IDA; AZRA; UNDP Resident Representative Office in Croatia; IMO; EIZ; Virovitica-Podravina County (VTC) Office for European Integration and Regional Development; CEPOR – SMEs and Entrepreneurship Policy Center; Chamber of Commerce (HGK) in Zagreb; Ministry of Foreign Affairs, Directorate for EU institutions and European Cooperation; World Bank – Croatia County Office; MELE, State Secretariate for Entrepreneurship: the European Commission Directorate General for Enlargement; the European Commission Directorate General for Regional Policy. The interviews were conducted at the last phase of a fieldwork process, following analysis of a range of primary and secondary documents. Interviews were conducted on the basis of individual anonymity and confidentiality with the aid of a semi-structured questionnaire with a mix of closed and open questions.
2. Multi-level governance refers to 'increasingly complex vertical relations between actors organized at various territorial levels and horizontal relations between actors from public, private and voluntary spheres' (Bache 2010).
3. Here we draw on the two types of multi-level governance developed by Marks and Hooghe (2004; see also Bache 2010). Type I multi-level governance describes system-wide governing arrangements in which the dispersion of authority is restricted to a limited number of clearly defined, non-overlapping jurisdictions at a limited number of territorial levels, each of which has responsibility for a 'bundle' of functions. By contrast, Type II multi-level governance describes governing arrangements in which the jurisdiction of authority is task-specific, where jurisdictions operate at numerous territorial levels and may be overlapping.
4. This document, alongside the Lisbon strategy, the Stabilization and Association Agreement and the National Programme for the Integration of the Republic of Croatia into the European Union, provided the basis for programming in Croatia.
5. The NUTS acronym originated from the French *nomenclature des unités territoriales statistiques*. The NUTS system provides a hierarchical categorization of different territorial units in the EU according to five levels, the largest being NUTS 1 (sections of a country

grouping together basic regions). This level was subdivided into NUTS 2 (basic regions), with subdivisions continuing through NUTS 3 and NUTS 4 to the smallest level of NUTS 5 (villages and towns). NUTS 2 regions, which were generally defined by member states for their own regional policy purposes, were the ones adopted for the main territorial objectives of cohesion policy. For practical reasons – that is the availability of suitable data – the NUTS categories were generally based on the existing institutional divisions within member states.

References

Bache, I. 2010. Europeanization and multi-level governance: EU cohesion policy and pre-accession aid in Southeast Europe. *Southeast European and Black Sea Studies* 10, no. 1: 1–12.

CODEF. 2006. *Strategic development framework for 2006–2013*. Ed. M. Dalic. http://www.strategija.hr.

CODEF. 2007. *Glossary of the European Union funds*. Ed. M. Dalic, N. Mikus, D. Cilic, and I. Maletic. http://www.strategija.hr.

European Commission. 2008. *674 Final: Croatia progress report 2008.* Brussels: European Commission.

Hughes, J., G. Sasse, and C. Gordon. 2002. *The ambivalence of conditionality: Europeanization and regionalization in Central and Eastern Europe.* ECPR Joint Sessions, March 22–27. Turin: ECPR.

Jacoby, W. 2005. External incentives and lesson-drawing in regional policy and health care. In *The Europeanization of Central and Eastern Europe*, ed. F. Schimmelfennig and U. Sedelmeier, 91–111. Ithaca, NY: Cornell University Press.

Kopric, I. 2004. Priority areas in reforming governance and public administration in Croatia. Paper presented at the UNPAN meeting on Priorities in Innovating Governance and Public Administration in the Euro-Mediterranean Region, May 17–20, in Napoli, Italy. http://unpan1.un.org/intradoc/groups/public/documents/un/unpan017009.pdf (accessed March 22, 2006).

Marcou, G. 2002. *Regionalization for development and accession to the European Union: A comparative perspective.* Budapest: Local Government and Public Service Reform Initiative.

Marks, G., and L. Hooghe. 2004. Contrasting visions of multi-level governance. In *Multi-level governance*, ed. I. Bache and M. Flinders, 15–30. Oxford: Oxford University Press.

Schmidt, V. 2006. *Democracy in Europe.* Oxford: Oxford University Press.

Stabilization and Association Agreement between the European Communities and their Member States, of the one part, and the Republic of Croatia, of the other part (SAA). *Official Journal of the European Union* 48: 1–222.

Sumpor, M. 2007. Is there any institutional capacity for integrated regional development? – Application of new governance approaches in Croatia. Paper presented at the 47th Congress of the European Regional Science Association, August 29–September 2, in Paris.

Zakosek, N. 2004. Das politische system Kroatiens [The political system of Croatia]. In *Die politischen Systeme Osteuropas*, ed. W. Ismayr, 677–726. Opladen: Leske and Budrich.

Europeanization and F.Y.R. Macedonia: towards a compound polity?

Gorica Atanasova[a] and Ian Bache[b]

[a]South East European Centre, City College Thessaloniki, University of Sheffield, Sheffield, UK; [b]Department of Politics, University of Sheffield, Sheffield, UK

This contribution considers whether European Union (EU) pre-accession aid is contributing to the development of a more compound polity in F.Y.R. Macedonia and, specifically, the extent to which there is a process of Europeanization characterized by emergent features of multi-level governance. After examining the state of play concerning governance and politics, the different EU pre-accession instruments are discussed with a focus on the Instrument for Pre-Accession Assistance. The main argument advanced is that F.Y.R. Macedonia is a simple polity that is quickly evolving into a compound polity and that the EU accession process and the requirements of pre-accession aid are important factors in this evolution process. However, alongside EU-induced changes are other initiatives and processes that are often promoting change in the same direction that make it increasingly difficult to isolate the independent effect of EU pressures.

Introduction

This contribution analyses the nature and extent of multi-level governance promoted in F.Y.R. Macedonia through the requirements of European Union (EU) pre-accession instruments, and particularly those that prepare the ground for eventual accession and administration of the structural funds and other instruments of EU cohesion policy. In doing so, it also explores the importance of other initiatives and processes that are often promoting change in the same direction, particularly in relation to decentralization, in order to come to a clearer assessment of the causal role of Europeanization (see Bache 2010).

After a brief 'Introduction', the article moves ahead with a discussion of the nature of governance and politics in F.Y.R. Macedonia, which is essentially a simple polity, but one that we suggest is evolving quickly in a more compound direction.[1] We then turn to a discussion of the EU instruments in F.Y.R. Macedonia, with a particular focus on the Instrument for Pre-Accession Assistance (IPA), which has most obvious resonance for research on multi-level governance (discussed below). The next section includes the main findings from the interviews and other research undertaken for this article.[2] It highlights the main developments that have taken place in relation to multi-level governance before considering the vertical and horizontal dimensions respectively.[3]

Our concluding section argues that while the effect of EU instruments on F.Y.R. Macedonia is relatively recent, there are still discernible effects on Type II multi-level governance[4] in particular. Moreover, while it is difficult to judge the lasting significance of these recent developments, the convergence of EU pressures and domestic priorities suggests ongoing moves in this direction in the foreseeable future.

Governance and politics in F.Y.R. Macedonia

The Republic of Macedonia is a relatively new and evolving democratic state that proclaimed its independence in 1991 and began the process of democratization on the ruins of the dissolved Yugoslav Federation. Historically, F.Y.R. Macedonia was a part of the Ottoman Empire, replaced by the Kingdom of Serbs, Croats and Slovenes (where it did not constitute an autonomous or administrative unit) which was superseded by the Yugoslav Federation.

The Yugoslav system was an unorthodox type of socialist regime due to the introduction of the self-management form of economic organization. The self-management system was marked by centralist administration and financing while allowing for some degree of regionalization and de-collectivization of property and agriculture. This arrangement, coupled with the selective and unequal distribution of funding from the centre, allowed for vast disparities between the states that lingered in the post-communist period.

While some of the states spent five centuries under the Ottoman Empire (Macedonia, Bosnia, Montenegro and parts of Serbia), others came out of the previous Austro-Hungarian rule (Slovenia, Croatia) which impacted on the ways of doing things and on the availability of resources. F.Y.R. Macedonia, being among the poorest and the smallest of the six states, received the least funding within the framework of Yugoslavia, thus becoming even poorer and less developed in comparison to the other states (US Department of State 2009). This lack of proper development under the former Yugoslavia complicated F.Y.R. Macedonia's difficult and thorny transition to democracy.

The modes of governance within the former Yugoslavia were also centralized in Belgrade. Hence, policy-making was made at the centre of the one-party system with the participation of Macedonian representatives of the Socialist Party. After the dissolution of the federation, although F.Y.R. Macedonia opted for independence, it found itself in a rather complex position: a sovereign, self-governed country had to be built, simultaneous with the development of a democratic system for which there was no historic precedent.

Post-Yugoslavia, F.Y.R. Macedonia had weak social structures independent of the state (Ivanov 2001) and the change of regime occurred only at the level of the political elites, with the vast majority of the population uninvolved. Studies have shown that no more than 1% of the Macedonian population was involved in the historical events in the beginning of the 1990s (Milosavlevski 1993, 144). Other social forces such as dissidents, labour unions or civil society actors were either weak or in the process of forming in this period and were not an effective counter to the power of the political elites, who were themselves offspring of the former Socialist Party. In short, the nation and state building processes coincided – and arguably collided – with democratization and transition in the social (and economic) spheres also.

After the establishment of the multi-party system in 1991, democratic practices were slowly developed, albeit in a centralized manner and executed by the existing socialist institutions. Yet, the institutional structure has not prevented political manoeuvring from hindering the process of democratic development. Moreover, changes of government have further undermined stability with abrupt changes in both political and administrative personnel and also in policy direction. The result has been a sporadic performance economically (growth, attracting foreign direct investments), politically (inter-ethnic issues, public administration, local self-governance) and socially (poverty and unemployment). Despite this record, the situation in F.Y.R. Macedonia, post-Yugoslavia, has at no time reached a point at which the role and functioning of the institutions has seriously threatened their eventual collapse.

Throughout this period, F.Y.R. Macedonia remained highly centralized. In the 1990s, centralized control was exercised over the 134 municipalities and no strategic efforts towards decentralization existed in the country, despite the existence of the *Strategy for Reform of the System of Local Self-governance in the Republic of Macedonia of 1999* (Taleski 2005, 9). A turning point was the signing of the Ohrid Framework Agreement (OFA), brokered by the EU and the USA, in the context of emerging inter-ethnic tension in F.Y.R. Macedonia. The OFA introduced consensual power-sharing modalities between the two major communities (Macedonian and Albanian) and paved the way for the development of regional policy (Taleski 2005, 9).

The OFA allowed for the introduction of constitutional amendments, laws on decentralization, a new territorial division of the country and the enactment of a law on local-self government. Subsequently, the number of municipalities was reduced from 134 to 84 and there was a significant transfer of competences from central to local government (e.g. management of primary education, social and medical services and all cultural activities; Taleski 2005, 9). Decentralization continued with the adoption of the Law on Balanced Regional Development in 2007, although this stemmed directly from EU requirements and the process of integration towards the EU (discussed below).

EU instruments in F.Y.R. Macedonia

F.Y.R. Macedonia is at a relatively early stage of accession towards the EU. It is part of the Stabilization and Association process designed for the Western Balkan countries that was reconfirmed at the Thessaloniki Summit in 2003 and the EU-Western Balkans Declaration (EU-Western Balkans Summit Declaration 2003, 1). It is a candidate country in preparation for obtaining a start date for accession negotiations. F.Y.R. Macedonia has received EU assistance under a broad range of programmes that have evolved from providing emergency assistance, reconciliation and stabilization, towards achieving a greater convergence with EU standards and legislation and, specifically of relevance here, for preparation for participation in EU cohesion policy post-accession. In financial terms, F.Y.R. Macedonia received more than €870 million of assistance from the EU between 1992 and 2007 (Commission of the European Communities 2008, 4). Here, we focus on those instruments with most relevance for our concern with multi-level governance.

F.Y.R. Macedonia became eligible for funding under Phare/Obnova[5] programme in 1996 following the extension of the programme to the countries of the Western Balkans. The programme aimed to strengthen public administration and institutions, promote convergence with EU legislation and prepare the country for the future participation in the EU cohesion policy. In 1999, Phare was extended with the introduction of two sector-specific programmes – the programme for rural and agricultural development (Sapard) and the programme for infrastructure projects in the area of environment and transport (ISPA).

Following the design of the Stabilization and Association process for the countries of the Western Balkans, the CARDS programme was introduced as the new financial instrument for political, economic and institutional stabilization and development. CARDS became operational in 2002 and was managed by the European Agency for Reconstruction (EAR) in the 2000–2006 timeframe. There were four priority areas for which CARDS assistance was provided to F.Y.R. Macedonia: democracy and the rule of law; justice and home affairs; economic and social development; and environment and natural resources (European Agency for Reconstruction 2002).

IPA

In January 2007, IPA replaced the previous pre-accession instruments. It incorporates five components: (1) transition assistance and institution building; (2) cross-border cooperation; (3) regional development; (4) human resources development; and (5) rural development. As a candidate country, F.Y.R. Macedonia is eligible for all five components and was set to receive around €300 million via IPA for the period 2007–2010 (Commission of the European Communities 2007). Co-financing for this period was estimated at around €80 million. Based on the assessment of strategic needs and priorities, the pre-accession assistance strategy for the period 2007–2009 is concentrated on four activity areas: institution building, cross-border cooperation, participation in the Community's cohesion policy, and rural development instruments and decentralized management of EU funds.

Of most direct relevance for our discussion, IPA provides the basis for future implementation of EU cohesion policy through the introduction of regional and rural development measures, as well as cross-border cooperation initiatives, through Components 2, 3 and 5, which was not the case with the previous instruments. To this end, it is implemented through multi-annual programmes that are aligned to the *Multi-annual Indicative Planning Document* developed by the European Commission in consultation with the national authorities, which incorporate the priorities for a three-year period.

A central aim of IPA is to transfer the management of assistance to the candidate countries to strengthen their ownership of the EU integration process. To this end, each candidate country has to establish a Decentralized Implementation System (DIS) – a national system for implementing IPA – in order for them to take control over the whole project cycle. Effectively, this system would meet the conditions for implementing the structural funds and related instruments post-accession, and so required F.Y.R. Macedonia to create new systems for programming, management, financial control, monitoring and evaluation, and to introduce the necessary legal, administrative and institutional adjustments.

At the time of our research (end 2008), F.Y.R. Macedonia had not secured DIS accreditation from the Commission, but was introducing a raft of measures in order to do so. Moreover, while DIS accreditation was required before IPA Components 3, 4 and 5 could be implemented, other measures under IPA Components 1 and 2, had begun. These measures could be initially managed at the national level.

Governance effects and domestic change

Key developments

The pace of change in response to pre-accession instruments and IPA in particular has been rapid, albeit uneven at times. F.Y.R. Macedonia has taken steps towards creating its own regional policy (below). It introduced regional structures according to NUTS criteria[6] in 2008, along with numerous mechanisms and processes through which to facilitate effective implementation of pre-accession aid, including a strategic coherence framework that sets the basis for the usage of EU funds over the seven-year period, 2007–2013.

The creation of a domestic regional policy and other significant initiatives came through the Law on Balanced Regional Development passed in May 2007. As one Ministry of Finance official (interview 2008) told us: 'We previously did not have an essential policy for balanced regional development. Due to this we have such a great lack of balance between Skopje and other places'. This led to the creation of planning regions and regional councils and the release of a small amount of central funding for this policy for the first time in 2007. At the national level, the Law created a Council for Regional Development comprising ministers and representatives from the regional councils, to coordinate regional policies. However, as discussed further below, at the time of our research the Law and the related bodies had not yet become fully operational.

Generally speaking, the widespread support for EU accession in F.Y.R. Macedonia is the key to understanding the pace of change in relation to features of multi-level governance. Domestic interviewees were of a shared view that 'the EU is the only game in town' and, as one government official put it, 'you cannot promote a system or a policy if it is not aligned with EU policies' (Secretariat for European Affairs official, interview 2009). Interviewees noted that over a relatively short period of time, there had been more cooperation between domestic institutions and international organizations as 'understanding has grown about what needs to be done and how it needs to be done' (Secretariat for European Affairs official, interview 2009). Although, again, we should not assume that this is without question and without exception. As one EAR official (interview 2009) put it: 'Domestic actors are receptive of the EU's role, but there are sometimes difficulties in having a relevant response from government. Sometimes it does not come at all: for example, co-financing for projects might not come'. Moreover, as this quotation indicates, the issue of compliance is not just about willingness, but also about capacity – in this case financial capacity – to respond. Similar comments were made by interviewees about capacity in relation to staff in key organizations: both in terms of numbers and relevant skills. A European Commission official put it slightly differently: 'sometimes there is commitment but not enough action!' (Commission Delegation to F.Y.R. Macedonia official, interview 2008). However, there was acknowledgement within the Commission that inter-ethnic issues and shifting political alliances in the governing coalition often meant there were complex internal debates and processes involved in shaping an appropriate response. Moreover, this was seen within the Commission to have positive aspects in promoting a culture of dialogue internally.

The main issue between the Commission and F.Y.R. Macedonia at the time of our research was that, despite the changes noted above, the Commission had not felt able to confer management power to national authorities for them to implement IPA funds in a decentralized manner. Once accreditation for DIS had been granted, national authorities would be responsible for tendering and contracting, with a degree of control maintained by the Commission, and in particular the Commission Delegation in Skopje.

In moving towards the decentralized management processes required by the EU, F.Y.R. Macedonia is drawing lessons from the experience of Turkey, Bulgaria and Croatia. However, as a number of interviewees reported, F.Y.R. Macedonia is the first state to be targeted for accreditation for DIS under IPA rather than Phare, and so while it is possible for lessons to be drawn from the experiences of other states, there are also additional requirements under IPA that make the Macedonian case unique. Commission officials indicated that progress was being made and identified lack of domestic capacity as the main obstacle. However, accreditation was expected to be conferred in 2009.

The vertical dimension of multi-level governance

At the beginning of the period of transition, national authorities feared that the secessionist and radical ideas of some individuals might divide the country to form a greater Albania or greater Serbia (Isakovic 1997). In the first phase of debates on decentralization, there were significant tensions and the first attempts to decentralize led to further ethnicization of the country because the new local units were drawn along ethnic lines by political elites taking decisions behind closed doors and without wide consultation. However, from the signing of the OFA onwards, the fear of decentralization among political elites has declined.

Despite this, F.Y.R. Macedonia remains a highly centralized country. While there is both internal and external support for decentralization, the reality is that the priority at this stage in the country's development tends to be on developing national capacity. This is true in relation to assistance through IPA, as one Commission official put it:

> It needs a strong inter-ministerial coordination at the level of the Ministry of Finance and the involvement of each line ministry: transport, environment, economy, regional development, education, labour, etc. Line ministries also have to draft operational programmes ... So planning, programming, it's really at the central level ... So the idea is really to reinforce, first, central government steering, planning, programming, implementation. And at a later stage can come the decentralization to the municipalities. (DG Regio official, interview 2008)

Yet, the multiple drivers for decentralization in force in F.Y.R. Macedonia mean that it is a process that is likely to remain prominent. However, while there is an EU element here in relation to both the OFA and pre-accession aid, we cannot attribute a strong causal influence to pre-accession aid requirements. Rather, we can suggest that the specific management requirements of IPA have begun to shape the nature of parts of the decentralization process to ensure that F.Y.R. Macedonia is equipped to successfully administer structural funds post-accession. For example, in direct response to EU requirements, F.Y.R. Macedonia created eight NUTS 3 regions[7] for the purposes of implementing the regional dimension of development policy.

These regions are overseen by new institutions – the Councils of the Planning Regions – which have been established by the mayors who participate in the given regions. These eight Councils were established in the Law on Balanced Regional Development. This is a significant change in the administration of development policy in F.Y.R. Macedonia. Once the Councils are fully functioning, they will consist of representatives of both the local and national levels and will thus constitute a partnership at a previously absent territorial level of governance. Moreover, the Councils would be required to consult with other stakeholders within the region in developing activities – including the municipalities, business representatives and NGOs.

While, at the time of our research, F.Y.R. Macedonia had to do more to satisfy the requirements for DIS, domestic interviewees were keen to explain some of the practical difficulties faced in meeting these requirements: 'there is commitment ... however, the country is for the first time undertaking such a serious effort' (Secretariat for European Affairs official, interview 2008). Moreover, these EU-influenced developments were broadly consistent with domestic objectives. As an official from the Ministry of Finance (interview 2008) reported:

> It is very important that we are for the first time putting in place a mechanism and system with the usage of a bottom-up approach, through engaging the municipalities by acquiring their ambitions, priorities, interests joined in planning regions and devising priorities as well as by having in mind the national priorities, national programmes, territorial plan of the country, to guide the municipalities in order to find a meeting point between the two – top and bottom priorities in order to come up with the joint national priorities for the planning regions.

The National Council for Regional Development had the responsibility for defining priorities and measures for domestic regional policy, but the Ministry for Local Self Government was also centrally involved and the relevant line ministries all consulted (along with other relevant stakeholders – see below). Once the priorities and measures were determined, the municipalities would have responsibility for implementation.

The horizontal dimension of multi-level governance

To the extent that there is horizontal coordination of activities in F.Y.R. Macedonia through pre-accession aid, it is not yet strong. Consultation rather than partnership is probably the best way to describe the nature of most cross-sectoral activity. Of course, this is not insignificant, particularly given the early stage of developments. On this issue, the EU and other international organizations are important. As one official from the European Agency for Reconstruction[8] (EAR) put it:

> No donor will devise a project without a consultation from domestic actors. There is consultation with civil society actors before the programming takes place in order to ensure their needs/objectives are taken into account and in the implementation process consultation between all stakeholders. This is to avoid redundancy of programmes and to make proposals which will be more need based. In the implementation phase, stakeholders are also involved. (Interview 2008)

Domestically, there was consultation over the development of the strategic coherence framework with the NGOs and other domestic actors, although this process was driven by central ministries. However, this in itself is seen as progress in F.Y.R. Macedonia, as in the early years of independence international organizations themselves prepared the documents. Now it is the government consulting the EU on drafting these documents rather than the other way around. Moreover, consultation with domestic actors was seen to be growing markedly, albeit starting from a low base.

As one EU delegation official (interview 2009) put it: 'cooperation is developing and this trend will continue in the future ... academia, trade unions and chambers of commerce were all involved equally and transparently'. The exception here was representation from the NGOs. The NGOs felt under-represented in some processes and, again, capacity issues were prominent. In addition, other interviewees suggested that the NGOs lacked umbrella organizations that could facilitate their integration into consultation processes more effectively. However, workshops and other activities were taking place to allow the NGOs to strengthen their role in the process, and IPA Component 1 was a funding mechanism for such activity. In this sense, and in relation to institution-building more generally, while other IPA components have a more direct relevance to the development of capacity for administering the structural funds post-accession, it is clear that other components are also relevant.

Consultations reveal areas of conflict, as well as broad support for EU goals. In relation to the strategic coherence framework, the disagreements were around which priorities and which areas were to be included for EU funding. A more specific example given was over whether economic development projects with respect for environmental protection should be given priority. Thus, the nature of the conflict in F.Y.R. Macedonia is not particularly dissimilar to the disagreements that have been found around the table at similar meetings across the EU where funding decisions have to be taken.

While the dominant form of cross-sectoral engagement is through consultation, attempts at constructing partnerships that are more durable and interdependent have begun. There is a sectoral monitoring committee (at the national level) for the IPA operational programme in which there are representatives from the municipalities, the association of local government units and the regional bodies. A Commission official suggested that there was a 'lively partnership' relating to this committee, while noting that the NGOs complained that they were not sufficiently involved (DG Regio official, interview 2008). However, in response to one complaint from the environmental NGOs, they had been given autonomy over the selection of their representative, which had initially been denied to them. As other components of IPA became operational, a monitoring committee would be established for each.

Again, it should be emphasized here that the processes of consultation and particular of partnership working are at an early stage in F.Y.R. Macedonia and, as one government official suggested to us, the real test of the consultation and partnership would come once the bulk of IPA had been released to F.Y.R. Macedonia following DIS accreditation. At this point, IPA would become 'a political issue *par excellence*' (Ministry of Finance official, interview 2008).

Discussion

F.Y.R. Macedonia is a country that is experiencing a difficult period of transition. There are important internal differences between different political factions and external disputes with neighbours. There is a lack of governing capacity and administrative expertise at both the central and local levels. There are serious economic and social issues, with high unemployment and large areas of under-development. These problems are compounded by problems of corruption and a high level of politicization. EU actors in particular raised the issue of politicization as a problem in F.Y.R. Macedonia, with one direct consequence being the relatively quick and abrupt turnover of personnel in key departments following a change of government. As one Commission official stated, 'the main problem is politicization. For example, people are changed because they don't belong to the ruling party, even though they are professional' (Delegation representative, interview 2009).

It is because of these difficult and complex problems that EU accession is so important to F.Y.R. Macedonia. It is generally viewed as 'the only way forward'. And it is only by understanding something of the nature of these problems alongside the enthusiasm to respond positively to the EU's agenda that we can understand the governance effects of pre-accession aid. There have been several notable developments to date, but it is too early to judge their significance with any certainty.

In terms of Type I multi-level governance, pre-accession aid has sought to develop capacity at both the central and local levels and in this sense is assisting the development of Type I bodies. Moreover, while it has focused primarily on the development of central government capacity in the first phase, it has also provided resources for the development of local capacity and, through its partnership requirement, increased cooperation between these levels of government. In addition, in direct response to EU requirements, a new intermediate tier of governance has been introduced at the NUTS 3 level, with the creation of regional planning councils.

In relation to Type II multi-level governance, there is again evidence of change. Within the central state, cross-departmental groups have been established (IPA units), as have various task-specific working groups. Another direct institutional response was the creation of the Central Financing and Control Unit to oversee the operational management of IPA. At the sub-national level, the creation of regional planning councils provides the clearest evidence of Type II developments.

Conclusion

In Schmidt's (2006) terms, F.Y.R. Macedonia constitutes a simple polity through its centralist legacy and statist policy-making processes. However, it is a polity in transition and, very often, turmoil. There is no doubt that our research points to a polity that is rapidly becoming more compound and that the EU is a key factor in this. The EU's effect works on two levels: through offering the prospect of membership and through specific policy requirements.

On the general level, accession to the EU is seen by Macedonian political elites and by the general public as the likeliest, if not only, route to democratization and development. F.Y.R. Macedonia's future as an independent nation is seen as most secure and most likely to flourish within the broader EU framework. This view stimulates a willingness to respond positively to EU requests. Yet at the same time, there are significant domestic barriers that mean that this response can fall short of what is required. Despite this, the net effect of the membership prospect has been domestic change that strengthens the prospects for multi-level governance in the country through incorporation of principles and practices that are aimed at strengthening governance at various territorial levels and at strengthening the capacity of non-state actors to participate in the policy process.

On the more specific level of pre-accession aid, we have observed a number of direct effects that have added to the complexity of the polity. At the national level, a monitoring committee for IPA has been established and others will follow; national ministries have reformed internally to allow them to participate in IPA programming and other activities; and cross-departmental units and other bodies have been created to improve coordination. At the sub-national level, a new regional tier has been created with accompanying bodies for overseeing strategic policy delivery; local councils have benefited from capacity-building funds and have been brought into consultation processes for programme development. Horizontally, there are new consultation processes that relate to various strategic documents that are often driven nationally but involve sub-national and non-state actors. Further, there are capacity-building measures aimed specifically at civil society groups to allow them to pursue a more effective role in policy-making.

At various stages in our discussion, we have been very tentative in our claims about the significance of developments. However, and here, we refer back directly to the opening contribution to this volume (Bache 2010), the timing of the intersection of the EU's pre-accession aid at this phase of F.Y.R. Macedonia's history does hold out the prospect of these changes having lasting significance. At the EU level, the changes to the pre-accession aid regime that were introduced in 2007 are significant in providing very clear requirements in relation to the administration of funding.

Unlike previous accessions, in this phase of EU enlargement, states such as F.Y.R. Macedonia will be fully expected to have in place the necessary structures and processes for delivering structural funding *before* acceding. These are structures and processes that resemble and promote multi-level governance. This point in the policy's evolution intersects with a point in domestic politics when fears relating to decentralization have receded and where other features of IPA relating to multi-level governance are either viewed positively or as a necessary corrective to failing domestic processes. Inevitably, some domestic actors will resist such changes where their position is threatened, but the forces in favour of change are currently greater.

Acknowledgements

This study draws on research funded by the UK Economic and Social Research Council (Multi-level Governance in Southeast Europe, ESRC grant no. RES-062-23-0183). We would like to thank the ESRC for its support and the two anonymous referees for the journal for their helpful comments on earlier versions of this article. All the usual disclaimers apply.

Notes

1. In a simple polity, power and influence are traditionally more concentrated in a single level and mode of governance. This categorization of states contrasts with that of compound polities, in which power and influence are diffused through multiple levels and modes of governance (Schmidt 2006).
2. In the period between January and September 2008, 18 semi-structured expert-interviews were conducted with representatives of the following organizations: Programming Unit, European Agency for Reconstruction Skopje; Sector for Coordination of Foreign Assistance, Secretariat for European Affairs/UNDP Macedonia; Sector for Coordination of Foreign Assistance, Secretariat for European Affairs; Delegation of the European Commission to Skopje; Operations-Infrastructure & Local Self-Government, European Agency for Reconstruction: IPA Coordination, Secretariat for European Affairs; Policy Coordination/ Coordination of Chapters 14, 21 and 22 of the EU Acquis, Secretariat for European Affairs; Sector for European Integration, Ministry of Foreign Affairs; IPA Management, EU Mission to Skopje; Ministry of Local-Self Government; Central Financing and Control Department, Ministry of Finance; the European Commission Directorate General for Enlargement; the European Commission Directorate General for Regional Policy. The interviews were conducted at the last phase of a fieldwork process, following an analysis of a range of primary and secondary documents. Interviews were conducted on the basis of individual anonymity and confidentiality with the aid of a semi-structured questionnaire with a mix of closed and open questions.

3. Multi-level governance refers to 'increasingly complex vertical relations between actors organized at various territorial levels and horizontal relations between actors from public, private and voluntary spheres' (Bache 2010).
4. Here, we draw on the two types of multi-level governance developed by Marks and Hooghe (2004; see also Bache 2010). Type I multi-level governance describes system-wide governing arrangements in which the dispersion of authority is restricted to a limited number of clearly defined, non-overlapping jurisdictions at a limited number of territorial levels, each of which has responsibility for a 'bundle' of functions. By contrast, Type II multi-level governance describes governing arrangements in which the jurisdiction of authority is task-specific, where jurisdictions operate at numerous territorial levels and may be overlapping.
5. The Obnova programme was an initiative of the European Commission for reconstruction and rehabilitation of the countries of the former Yugoslavia.
6. Nomenclature of Territorial Units for Statistics. The NUTS acronym originated from the French *nomenclature des unités territoriales statistiques*. The NUTS system provides a hierarchical categorization of different territorial units in the EU according to five levels, the largest being NUTS 1 (sections of a country grouping together basic regions). This level was subdivided into NUTS 2 (basic regions), with subdivisions continuing through NUTS 3 and NUTS 4 to the smallest level of NUTS 5 (villages and towns). NUTS 2 regions, which were generally defined by member states for their own regional policy purposes, were the ones adopted for the main territorial objectives of cohesion policy. For practical reasons – i.e. the availability of suitable data – the NUTS categories were generally based on the existing institutional divisions within member states.
7. At the EU level, F.Y.R. Macedonia as a whole forms one NUTS 2 statistical region.
8. EAR is an independent agency of the EU, which managed a number of reconstruction related projects in F.Y.R. Macedonia and the wider Western Balkans region. The mandate of the Agency expired in 2008 and it terminated its activities.

References

Bache, I. 2010. Europeanization and multi-level governance: EU cohesion policy and pre-accession aid in Southeast Europe. *Southeast European and Black Sea Studies* 10, no. 1: 1–12.

Commission of the European Communities. 2007. *Commission Decision C (2007) 1853 of 30/04/2007 on a Multi-annual Indicative Planning Document (MIPD) 2007–2009 for the former Yugoslav Republic of Macedonia.* http://ec.europa.eu/enlargement/pdf/mipd_fyrom_2007_2009_en.pdf.

Commission of the European Communities. 2008. *Commission Decision of on a Multi-annual Indicative Planning Document (MIPD) 2008–2010 for the former Yugoslav Republic of Macedonia.* http://ec.europa.eu/enlargement/pdf/mipd_fyrom_ 2008_2010_en.pdf.

European Agency for Reconstruction. 2002. *Country strategy paper for the F.Y.R. Macedonia 2002–2006: CARDS assistance programme.* http://ec.europa.eu/enlargement/archives/ear/fyrom/fyrom.htm.

EU-Western Balkans Summit Declaration. 2003. *European Commission, Enlargement 2003. EU-Western Balkans Summit Declaration.* Thessaloniki Summit. http://ec.europa.eu/enlargement/enlargement_process/accession_process/how_does_a_country_join_the_eu/sap/thessaloniki_summit_en.htm.

Isakovic, Z. 1997. *International position of Macedonia and Balkan security.* Copenhagen Peace Research Institute. http://www.uottawa.ca/associations/balkanpeace/texts/isakovic-macedonia97.html.

Ivanov, G. 2001. The power of the powerless: Democracy and civil society in Macedonia. In *Democratic reconstruction in the Balkans*, ed. M. Blunden and P. Burke, 67–82. London: Centre for the Study of Democracy, University of Westminster.

Marks, G., and L. Hooghe. 2004. Contrasting visions of multi-level governance. In *Multi-level governance*, ed. I. Bache and M. Flinders, 15–30. Oxford: Oxford University Press.

Milosavlevski, S. 1993. *Istochna Evropa pomegu Egalitarizmot i Demokratijata* [East Europe between egalitarianism and democracy]. Skopje: Ljuboten.

Schmidt, V. 2006. *Democracy in Europe: The impact of European integration.* Cambridge: Cambridge University Press.

Taleski, D. 2005. *Decentralisation in the Republic of Macedonia: The last steps across the abyss.* Berlin: German Institute for International and Security Studies.

US Department of State. 2009. *Diplomacy in action. Background note: Macedonia.* http://www.state.gov/r/pa/ei/bgn/26759.htm.

Europeanization and multi-level governance in Turkey

Ebru Ertugal

Department of International Relations and the EU, Izmir University of Economics, Sakarya Cad. No. 156, 35330 Balcova, Izmir, Turkey

This study considers whether European Union (EU) pre-accession instruments relating to cohesion policy are contributing to the development of a more compound polity in Turkey and, specifically, assesses the extent to which Europeanization promotes features of multi-level governance. Empirical findings suggest that the implementation system for EU pre-accession aid is centralized with signs of a limited shift towards multi-level governance. Empirical findings also reveal that the implementation structures designed for national policy in response to EU requirements represent a greater degree of shift towards multi-level governance. The argument developed is that the latter is potentially transformative in character as far as regional development policy-making is concerned, though the Turkish polity is to date only slightly more compound as a consequence.

Introduction

Following the framework set out in the opening contribution to this volume (Bache 2010), this study considers the extent to which European Union (EU) pre-accession instruments relating to cohesion policy are contributing to the development of more compound polity in Turkey and, specifically, promoting multi-level governance.[1] The next section provides a brief background on the nature of governance and politics in Turkey, while the third section gives an overview of the relevant pre-accession instruments that have operated in Turkey. The fourth section provides an account of the main developments with respect to multi-level governance followed by an examination of vertical and horizontal dimensions, respectively, and the fifth section traces the causal process and disentangles the roles played by the EU and domestic factors in domestic change.

The argument developed is that while the implementation system for EU pre-accession aid is centralized with signs of a modest shift towards multi-level governance, the implementation structures designed for national policy in response to EU requirements are potentially transformative in character.

Governance and politics in Turkey

In terms of the basic distinction between simple and compound polities (Bache 2010), Turkey fits into a simple polity ideal type. Despite having a geographical size almost as big as France and Germany combined, Turkey's political and administrative structures have remained highly centralized for the most part of its modern history. The system of a centralized polity based on a unitary state and statist policy-making processes characterize Turkey's tradition of statehood.

The strong tradition of a highly centralized state is associated with the Turkish Republic's anxiety since its foundation in 1923 in maintaining national unity in the face of political Islam and ethnic separatism (Cizre-Sakallıoğlu 1997; Heper 1991). The state elite, in particular, the office of the president and the Constitutional Court function as key veto players through their jurisdiction over safeguarding the territorial integrity and national unity of the country (Heper 1990). The Constitutional Court has authority to check the constitutionality of laws and regulations upon referral by the president (or by one-fifth of the members of parliament).

As a reflection of its centralized polity, Turkey's territorial public administration consists of two levels: central and local (provincial). A meso (regional) level of public administration has not been formed because of the fear that the wider geographical area of a region might include a dominant ethnic group endangering the unity and security of the nation.[2] The centre–local territorial administration with the absence of a regional tier is strongly entrenched in Turkey's constitution. The local level consists of 81 provinces that are governed through a dual structure: on the one hand, there are provincial administrations headed by centrally appointed governors who at the same time chair the provincial assemblies which are directly elected. On the other hand, there are the directly elected (metropolitan) municipalities, whose numbers and size vary from province to province depending on population size. A characteristic feature of Turkey's governing system at the local level has been the absence of coordinating mechanisms among these public and local authorities (Güler 1998, 197).

Processes of public policy-making, including regional policy, have been isolated from civil society due to the weakness of connections between political parties and social groups in Turkey. The concentration of power at the centre and the control of the society through the distribution of patronage to local persons of influence have been important aspects of Turkey's state tradition (Danielson and Keleş 1985, 99; Kalaycioğlu 2001; Sunar 1994). This in turn prevented the tackling of distributional issues, including regional disparities, by direct instruments (Cizre-Sakallioğlu and Yeldan 2000, 500; Waldner 1999).

By the start of the 2000s, restructuring the administrative system had been on the agenda in Turkey for the last 40 years. At the same time, international organizations with which Turkey formed close relations (such as the International Monetary Fund, the Organisation for Economic Co-operation and Development and the World Bank) have been emphasizing (local) decentralization. However, the increasing level of ethnic separatist terrorism coupled with the increasing political Islamic activism in the 1980s and 1990s constituted crucial 'constraints' on domestic change.

In the meantime, the dissatisfaction with the prevailing centralized administrative system and clientelist politics have led to the formation of informal bottom-up regional networks in some of the more developed regions since the 1990s. These networks are often led by local business associations and local non-governmental organizations (NGOs) in an attempt to generate regional economic development in the face of perceived ineffectiveness of central government and dwindling public investments. Such regional networks have been more pronounced in more developed Aegean and Mediterranean regions.

In sum, governance and politics in Turkey stand in sharp contrast to the complex compound polity of the EU. In principle, this high degree of 'misfit' between EU and domestic governance can lead to considerable adaptational pressures (Bache 2010). However, domestic stability and continuity characterizing Turkey's political institutions (in contrast to the post-communist transition in other (former) candidate countries) leads to the expectation that the process of domestic change is likely to be slow, difficult and limited.

The relevant pre-accession instruments

Turkey had in place a domestic regional policy before it was confronted with EU requirements with the decision of the Helsinki European Council in December 1999, which admitted Turkey as an official candidate.[3] Domestic regional policy was formulated by the central administration (i.e. the State Planning Organization – SPO) based on the channelling of public investments and incentives for the private sector to key provincial towns. Regional plans, formulated by the SPO for a few regions determined in an ad hoc manner, remained devoid of implementation structures, though steps are being taken to address this major deficiency (discussed below).

The pre-accession instruments available to Turkey have changed over time due to system-wide changes in EU funding. Between 1996 and 2001, Turkey was included in the EU's financial instrument (MEDA) for the implementation of the Euro-Mediterranean Partnership. Instruments related to cohesion policy started to operate in Turkey under the pre-accession instrument in 2001. EU funds programmed between 2001 and 2006 aimed at promoting the adoption of the EU *acquis*, administrative capacity building, and economic and social cohesion. The total amount of funds Turkey received was €126 million in 2002, €145 million in 2003, €236 million in 2004, €277 million in 2005 and €450 million in 2006 (CEC 2007a, 7). During this period, EU funds for economic and social cohesion amounted to €461 million (CEC 2007a, 7). Regionally focused programmes were concentrated in 12 of the 26 NUTS 2 regions (put in place under EU pressure in 2002)[4] with a per capita income below 75% of the Turkish national average.

In the new programming period for 2007 and 2013, EU financial assistance in candidate countries is governed by the Instrument for Pre-Accession Assistance (IPA) which is made up of five components. Among those, Components 3 (regional development) and 4 (human resources) under IPA envisage centralized implementation structures in comparison to the pre-accession instrument. Under Component 3, the regional competitiveness operational programme and, under Component 4, the human resources development operational programme concentrate on the least developed 12 NUTS 2 regions. Under all five components, IPA provides a total of €497.2 million for 2007, €538.7 for 2008, €566.4 million for 2009, €653.7 million for 2010 and €781.9 for 2011 (CEC 2007b). When compared to the level of pre-accession funding for the Central and Eastern European countries, the ratio of EU funds available for Turkey may be as little as 1:10 in terms of per capita figures.[5] Therefore, IPA funds for Turkey are *scarce* 'in relation to Turkey's economic development needs' (CEC 2007a, 12).

The nature and extent of domestic change

Key developments

Domestic changes triggered in response to EU pre-accession requirements relating to cohesion policy fall into two distinct categories in Turkey: changes for the purpose of implementing EU funds and changes for the purpose of implementing national funds. This section gives an overview of both kinds of domestic change with a particular focus on those aspects most relevant to Type I and Type II multi-level governance.[6]

Under the pre-accession instrument between 2001 and 2006, the implementation of EU-funded regional programmes in 12 NUTS 2 regions required partnership between public actors at the central and regional levels. The main actors at the central level included: the General Directorate of Regional Development and Structural Adjustment within the SPO (the 'beneficiary' and the managing authority) and the newly created Central Finance and Contracts Unit set up in 2002 by a Memorandum of Understanding between the European Commission and Turkish government (an independent body but otherwise attached to the Secretariat General for EU Affairs and the Undersecretariat of Treasury). The Central Finance and Contract Unit's role concerned the budgeting, tendering, contracting and payments aspects of EU funds. The main actors at the regional level were the newly created Programme Implementation Units (PIUs) formed under the service unions, which were set up at NUTS 2 level by provincial administrations headed by provincial governors. Municipalities and village administrations could become members of service unions if they wanted.

Partnerships engendered between the SPO and PIUs for technical implementation and monitoring of EU-funded regional programmes proved to be effective as indicated by the high level of commitment rates (SPO 2007).[7] At the regional level, PIUs were responsible for effective programme implementation in compliance with EU procedures under the coordination of the SPO. The former organized information days and trainings about project preparation and management at the local level and were responsible for the coordination of technical assistance and monitoring. Service unions provided the facilities, personnel and resources of PIUs. Due to lack of local human resources, the majority of PIU personnel was appointed by provincial administrations from among civil servants working for local organizations of the central administration, which operate under the coordination of provincial governors.

Under IPA, regional competitiveness and human resources development operational programmes for 2007–2010 were prepared by the Ministry of Industry and Trade and the Ministry of Labour and Social Security, respectively, which constitute the operational structures responsible for management and implementation. These two operational programmes are precursors to structural funds embodying the principles of partnership and programming. However, their administration is at the national level rather than regional.

The SPO ensures strategic coordination between the two operational programmes through a Strategic Coherence Framework, which identifies more detailed priorities including business and enterprise support, and increased levels of labour force participation and human resources. Other IPA bodies at the central level include the Undersecretariat of Treasury which functions as the National Fund and the Secretary General for EU Affairs which is the National IPA Coordinator. Each operational programme has a sectoral monitoring committee that involves representatives from economic and social partners as well as representatives from IPA bodies and sectoral policy-making bodies. The sectoral monitoring committee for regional competitiveness operational programme additionally involves regional partners on a rotational basis.

Separate from the implementation of EU funds, the Turkish parliament passed new legislation in 2006 which establishes 26 regional development agencies (RDAs) to correspond to each of the 26 NUTS 2 regions in order to implement national funds. The SPO had started the preparations for the draft law in 2003. Following its adoption, the new law was subsequently challenged in the Constitutional Court. The ensuing legal battle was eventually resolved in favour of the new law (Law no. 5449), which came into effect at the end of 2008. Although not part of the public administration, RDAs institutionalized a nation-wide regional level in Turkey for regional development purposes for the first time.

For various reasons, the RDAs should be understood primarily as Type II multi-level governance bodies, though they have some Type I characteristics (below). First, they are task-specific, with key competences in the preparation and implementation of regional development plans and programmes, the monitoring and evaluation of these programmes, the promotion of cooperation among public and private sectors and NGOs to achieve regional development objectives and the provision of support to local level planning (SPO, Secretariat General for EU Affairs – EUSG, development agencies and EU officials, interviews 2008 and 2009) (OJ 2006). Second, the RDAs are also designed to be flexible in that they are subject to private law in order to enable them to respond freely to changing circumstances – when compared with public institutions – in coordinating the formation of local and regional networks. Third, in terms of membership, the decision-making body (i.e. the executive board) of the RDAs consists of local level representatives – including centrally appointed provincial governors, heads of directly elected provincial assemblies and directly elected mayors as well as presidents of local chambers of commerce and/or industry (OJ 2006). Therefore, membership at local and regional levels overlaps.

The vertical dimension of multi-level governance

Central government administration and ministries are the key actors in the implementation of EU funds. The Ministry of Industry and Trade and the Ministry of Labour and Social Security, as operating structures for the regional competitiveness and human resources operational programmes, and the SPO, as the strategic coordinator, have pivotal roles in domestic networks. In the drafting stage of the operational programmes, a working group for the regional competitiveness operational programme and two high-level and technical committees for human resources operational programme were set up. The purpose of these was to start the process of partnership consultation with stakeholders from public institutions and NGOs represented at the central level and with regional and local partners from targeted NUTS 2 regions, who were invited to take part in the preparations of the operational programmes (HRD-OP 2007; RCOP 2007).

Under regional competitiveness and human resources operational programmes, the instruments available do not significantly strengthen the vertical dimension of multi-level governance or promote a 'regionalization' in state structures that typify compound polities (Bache 2010). The sectoral monitoring committees meet at least twice a year and, so far, three meetings have taken place for each operational programme. The committees consist of representatives from central IPA bodies, sectoral policy-making bodies (i.e. line ministries), economic and social partners organized at the central level and regional partners. In the sectoral monitoring committee of the regional competitiveness operational programme, the participation of regional and local actors (governors, universities and chambers of industry and commerce) is provisional and subject to rotation. A 'rotating participation plan' is devised to give opportunity to local and regional partners from 43 provinces in 12 NUTS 2 regions to take part in the sectoral monitoring committee.

On the basis of sectoral monitoring committee meetings held so far for the regional competitiveness operational programme in particular, it is possible to observe that the influence of the regional actors has been limited and that they suffer from lack of familiarity with complicated EU funding procedures (SPO and EUSG officials, interviews 2009).[8] Despite the involvement of the targeted regions in the implementation of EU funding in the previous period, the turnover of officials at the governorates hampers the learning process. The fact that sectoral monitoring meetings held were conducted in English with no translation constituted an additional obstacle for exerting influence. Moreover, some of the regional partners could not take part in the meetings, which were held in Ankara, due to technical delays which prevented the funding of participants' travel expenses. The representation of regional partners on a rotational basis brings in an element of discontinuity, which may slow down their learning process and hence their ability to exert influence in comparison to economic and social partners organized at the central level. However, the newly formed structures for the purpose of implementing national funds – the RDAs – promote the vertical dimension of multi-level governance to a greater extent due mainly to the institutionalization of a nation-wide regional level of governance.

In terms of jurisdictional levels, the RDAs each correspond neatly to one NUTS 2 region with no overlaps in their jurisdictional areas – a feature of Type I multi-level governance. There is no non-incorporated area; consequently, all the country will be governed in regional development policy by a respective RDA. Multi-level governance is thus organized neatly at the local, regional and national levels. The vision of collective action encouraged by the RDAs is more than an 'instrumental arrangement' to 'solve *ad hoc* coordination problems' (Marks and Hooghe 2004, 28). Rather, the RDAs involve quasi-permanent non-intersecting jurisdictions, which may encourage identities with a particular 'region' in time and thus potential longer-term implications for the system-wide governance architecture.

The creation of RDAs strengthens considerably the vertical dimension of multi-level governance, which has historically been extremely weak in Turkey. The RDAs will intensify both interactions and interdependence between actors based at national, regional and local levels. On the one hand, in a number of respects the central administration continues to exercise power and authority over RDAs (OJ 2006). First, the legal basis of RDAs is not guaranteed in the constitution as the law on RDAs is a framework law. For the establishment of each RDA, a decision by the Council of Ministers is required. It is therefore possible that the Council of Ministers may take a decision later to close down RDAs, which means that the process is not irreversible. In practice, however, once established it would be politically highly costly to withdraw resources from vested local interests (SPO, EUSG, development agencies and EU officials, interviews 2008 and 2009).

Second, the heads of the RDAs are provincial governors. Moreover, the general-secretaries, responsible for day-to-day management, are selected by the SPO from among a list of candidates proposed by the RDAs. Third, regional plans and strategies formulated by the RDAs have to be approved by the SPO. The latter is responsible for evaluating RDA performance, which gives the SPO power in setting the agenda. Fourth, the RDAs are dependent on the central administration for the bulk of their resources. New arrangements, therefore, do not affect the power and authority of the state.

On the other hand, in contrast to the previous period, when most activity was monopolized by the centre, new structures create an opportunity for regional and local levels to exercise real influence over outcomes. First, the RDAs have informational advantages over central administration in the formulation of regional plans in such a geographically large and diverse country. It is for this reason that the central administration could never formulate regional plans for every region at any one time in the past, and when it did formulate regional plans for a few regions, most of those plans could not be implemented (Tekeli 2007; SPO 2000). It is therefore expected that the approval of regional plans by the SPO will be for the purposes of ensuring their conformity with national strategies and for providing overall coordination (SPO, EUSG and development agencies' officials, interviews 2008 and 2009).

Second, allocating national funds for the first time to regions (0.5% of the general budget) on a regular basis opens up a new focus of activity for local and regional actors for affecting regional development. Third, and most important, the RDAs will have autonomy in implementation. National funds will be administered by them according to a grant scheme in which they will both determine the project selection criteria (subject to approval by the SPO) and act as contracting authorities as well as decide individual applications (OJ 2008a). The RDAs will additionally be responsible for monitoring in partnership with the SPO (OJ 2008a).

Such authority, non-existent at the regional level in the previous period, creates a high degree of interdependence between national, regional and local levels for the successful implementation of regional plans and strategies. This interdependence is also reinforced indirectly through the local organizations of the central administration (line ministries such as the Ministry of Industry or the Ministry of Tourism), whose activities are coordinated by governors at the local level, who in turn are members of the executive boards of the RDAs. The Ministry of Interior is also indirectly involved through its administrative tutelage over governorates and its responsibility to oversee the external auditing of RDAs together with the Ministry of Finance. Overall, direct and indirect mechanisms of vertical policy coordination suggest much stronger multi-level governance in the vertical dimension when compared to the past.

The horizontal dimension of multi-level governance

Given that Turkey's public policy-making tradition has been statist, the most important effect of the implementation of EU funds under IPA has been the institutionalization of formal participation of economic and social partners, as well as regional partners, at the central level, that is 'pluralizing' effects in the simple–compound polity discourse. In particular, through their participation on a permanent basis in the sectoral monitoring committees, social and economic partners have gained an important potential opportunity to exercise influence in the programming and implementation of operational programmes. On the basis of sectoral monitoring committee meetings held so far, it can be observed that the influence of economic and social partners has suffered from lack of familiarity with complicated EU funding procedures (SPO and EUSG officials, interviews 2009). However, the strong interest shown in the meetings indicates that economic and social partners are going through a learning process which will enable them to be in a much better position to exert influence in the next programming of operational programmes for 2010–2013.

A characteristic feature of Turkey's public administration has been its fragmented nature with lack of coordination between various public institutions at the central level. In this context, another observation on the basis of sectoral monitoring committee meetings is that the EU's impact has been greatest in promoting cooperation and coordination between public institutions at the central level, which are well represented in the sectoral monitoring committees (SPO and EUSG officials, interviews 2009). Public institutions have been more dominant in these meetings in terms of influence due to their central role in the implementation of EU funds and their prior experience in administering EU funds in the previous programming period.

While implementation structures for EU funds promote the horizontal dimension of multi-level governance at the central level, new RDAs for implementing national funds promote the horizontal dimension (i.e. 'pluralizing' effects), at the regional level. Moreover, the RDAs will increase horizontal interactions and interdependence between local actors from different sectors at the regional level due to two main reasons (OJ 2006). First, the RDAs for the first time formally institutionalize cooperation at the regional level between public institutions (provincial governorates), local authorities (provincial assemblies and municipalities) and the private sector (local chambers of commerce and industry) through the decision-making body, that is the executive board. Further, the executive boards in three 'metropolitan' regions composed of one province only (i.e. Istanbul, Ankara and Izmir) also involve three representatives from the private sector and/or NGOs. The latter are elected by the development councils, which constitute advisory bodies of RDAs, composed of 100 representatives from public institutions, private sector, NGOs and universities in the regions (OJ 2006). The role of the development councils is advisory in that it is up to the executive board to take the former's recommendations into account. This suggests that the practice is likely to differ from region to region. In regions with a tradition of informal network formation among local actors, such as in the Aegean or the Mediterranean, it is expected that the development councils will be more vocal and able to exert more influence over decisions of the executive board (SPO and development agencies' officials, interviews 2008 and 2009).

Second, the national funds allocated to RDAs will be administered according to a grant scheme which is a novel way of ensuring that investments are sustained and of mobilizing local actors for collective action by providing incentives to access resources. Therefore, the horizontal dimension of multi-level governance is promoted considerably through the executive boards of RDAs and the grant scheme to be implemented. Furthermore, there is room for further influence over outcomes by economic and social partners represented in the development councils of RDAs depending on the dynamics of pre-existing traditions of cooperation and specific development problems in each region.

The role of central government

While there is change in both the vertical and horizontal dimensions of multi-level governance through EU policies, this is not yet undermining the role, power and authority of central state actors. Rather, the role of the state in regional policy and development is going through significant change as the governing context changes. Whereas previously, the state proved to be ineffective in formulating and implementing a nation-wide regional plan and strategy in a highly centralized polity, the new arrangements provide the opportunity to increase state effectiveness in a policy area in which the sheer size and diversity of the country matters to a great extent.

Tracing the causes of domestic change

While the expectation presented at the outset suggested a likely shift towards a more 'compound' polity, involving a process of slow, difficult and limited domestic change, the analysis above suggests that significant domestic change has taken place in a relatively short period of time without being prevented by veto players. It also suggests that the extent of domestic change, in particular with regards to the implementation structures for national policy, is more extensive than mere adaptation to the EU in order to qualify for EU funds.

The EU plays a direct role as far as implementation structures for EU funds are concerned. However, the EU's role is more indirect as far as the RDAs are concerned given that the latter implement national funds. However, while the EU's effect is indirect in relation to the creation of RDAs, it is by no means insignificant: their creation was the consequence of a coincidence of EU requirements for regional structures with a particularly conducive domestic context, that is the crucial significance of 'timing' (Bache 2010). The favourable domestic context was based on two domestic factors: the formation of a majority government with no ideological opposition to decentralization and the recognition of policy failure on the part of the bureaucrats at the SPO. In this domestic context, the EU's requirements for regionalization – and for participation and programming – served both the political interests of the government and the policy-learning needs of bureaucrats.

Following more than a decade of coalition governments, the Justice and Development Party (JDP) formed a single-party government with a comfortable majority to pass laws in parliament in 2002 (and again in 2007). The electoral success of the JDP represented the culmination of electoral success of its predecessor political parties at the local level over an extended period of time since the 1990s.

The political power of the JDP at the local level coupled with its Islamic roots distinguishes it from other mainstream political parties with regards to its position vis-à-vis decentralization. Not inhibited by fears of political Islam and aided, ironically, by a simple polity, one of the first things that the JDP government embarked upon was local government reform. Reform of the public administration had already been on the political agenda since the 1960s but had not been realized due to lack of political willingness. The Draft Law on the Basic Principles and Re-structuring of Public Administration, which was adopted by the parliament in July 2004, was subsequently vetoed by the then president for violating the unitary nature of the state.[9]

The Draft Law on the Basic Principles and Re-structuring of Public Administration envisaged far-reaching changes in centre–local relations introducing 'subsidiarity' in place of centralization. It also aimed to introduce regulatory local government to facilitate the mobilization of local resources and formation of local development coalitions (Şengül 2003, 203). This latter function of the law was seen as a response to the processes of globalization in general and requirements of international organizations – stand-by agreements with the IMF and conditions of credits obtained from World Bank – in particular (Güler 2003). Due to the presidential veto, the government attempted to pass separately the component legislations of the draft law from the parliament. Some of this legislation was adopted by the president but some of it was vetoed due to similar concerns.

The JDP government had also included legislation on RDAs into the package of public administration reforms. However, RDA legislation was quickly withdrawn due to deep sensitivities over the term 'region'. The reasons for the JDP's interest in RDAs stem not only from its lack of opposition to decentralization in general, but also from potential political gains to be made at local and regional levels in particular.

Two groups of political gains for the government can be distinguished (SPO, EUSG and EU officials, interviews 2008 and 2009). First, the political power of the JDP is expected to increase further at the local level through the channelling of public money, hitherto not available, through the RDAs. Second, the RDAs constitute visible and internationally recognized tools for addressing regional development. They create a strong impression that the government is attacking regional disparities at a time of growing demand by local actors to take part in the policy process affecting regional development.

'Thin learning' based on rational calculations on the part of politicians in power has been accompanied by an ongoing process of 'thick learning' in the SPO (Bache 2010). The challenge for the bureaucrats was one of developing a nation-wide approach to regional planning, rather than the hitherto ad hoc approach, and involving local people in the preparation of plans. However, the growing recognition of the need to address regional disparities[10] through regional planning was hampered by lack of know-how concerning the integration of regional plans into national plans and also by lack of implementation structures.

Lack of know-how is associated with national planning processes that are based on sectoral considerations and exclude the spatial distribution of economic activities from policy analysis (Tekeli 2007). It is through annual programmes of public investment projects prepared individually by various ministry organizations that national plans are carried out. In deciding annual programmes, interdependencies among individual projects are not considered. The issue of horizontal coordination between the line ministries and the SPO for regional planning is entangled with questions of what the status of the SPO is vis-à-vis the ministries and inter-institutional power balance, which could not be resolved in favour of coordination (Tekeli 1972). Furthermore, due to the annual nature of programmes, it is common for multi-annual investments to be discontinued subject to budget cuts.

Lack of implementation structures is associated with a technical approach to planning. Since planning and implementation are not considered together, potential feedback effects are prevented from informing the planning process. There has also been ambiguity as to whether the powers required for implementing structures, involving expenditure by a regional authority, could be achieved through a new law without necessitating a constitutional change (Tekeli 1972).

The EU requirements on regional policy provided answers to questions of lack of know-how and lack of implementation structures at a time when these problems had become acute (SPO 2000). First, the multi-annual programming and the grant scheme at the regional level provide ways of integrating regional plans into the national plan (SPO officials, interviews 2008 and 2009). Even though the nature of investments is smaller-scale in a grant scheme, the local stakeholders feel that once their project proposal is approved, its completion is guaranteed and not dependent on budget cuts that are outside their control (SPO and development agencies' officials, interviews

2008 and 2009). Rather than passively wait for public investments which may never materialize and over which local people have no say, the grant scheme operated by the RDAs promises a continuous and regular, albeit limited, flow of resources to the regions that local stakeholders can use.

Second, the fact that the RDAs (rather than 'regional authorities') are implementing the grant scheme depoliticizes the nature of change and provides for a relatively easier way of getting round veto players. Third, the RDAs address the issue of involving local stakeholders in policy processes, the concern for which was clear in the preparation of the second master plan for the Southeast Anatolia region in 2000, when participation remained non-institutionalized, ad hoc and weak (GAP 2002).

When Turkey was confronted with EU conditionality in regional policy, the 'timing' was thus right for both politicians in government and the SPO bureaucrats to embrace the implied changes for multi-level governance albeit in a manner that was politically feasible and that did not overtly challenge the unitary state, that is through 'layering' (Bache 2010). Upon political direction signalled by the government, the SPO started preparing the RDA draft law in 2003, which was adopted by the parliament in 2006. In order to avoid a potential veto, the Regional Development and Structural Adjustment General Directorate within the SPO engaged in intensive lobbying with the then president at the time of parliamentary adoption (SPO officials, interviews 2008 and 2009). Following the legal challenge by the parliamentary opposition party which referred the new law to the Constitutional Court, the SPO engaged in a similar process of persuading the Court. The new law finally entered into force in 2008 following the favourable decision of the Constitutional Court, which conceded the desirability to acquire the necessary public policy instruments that increase institutional capacity to address regional disparities (OJ 2008b).

Conclusion

This study has examined the multi-level governance effects of EU pre-accession aid requirements in Turkey. In the terminology of Europeanization research, Turkey provides a high 'degree of misfit' with EU requirements and generates the expectation of a slow and difficult process of domestic change towards a more compound direction. However, the analysis shows that the 'degree of misfit' is subject to interpretation and that significant domestic change has taken place within a relatively short time.

The study demonstrates that the impact of the EU requirements on multi-level governance can be observed in two domains: implementation structures designed for EU funds and related implementation structures designed for national funds. It argues that while the implementation system for EU pre-accession aid is centralized with signs of a modest shift towards multi-level governance, the implementation structures designed for national policy in response to EU requirements are potentially transformative in character.

The findings suggest that the extent of domestic change in the implementation arrangements for national policy in Turkey has been greater than expected. The newly created RDAs advance both the vertical and the horizontal dimensions of multi-level governance, that is both 'regionalization' and 'pluralization', with respect to regional development policy-making and implementation structures. The degree of domestic change goes beyond mere adaptation to EU requirements to qualify for EU funds. The

RDAs fit imperfectly into Type II multi-level governance because they incorporate some features of Type I as well. The formation of the RDAs corresponding neatly to each and every NUTS 2 region suggests that important changes are under way in Turkey, which is characterized by the stability of its institutions and a strong historical tradition of statehood. Viewed from this perspective, the effects of domestic change in Turkey are potentially transformative.

The explanation for the extent of domestic change provided by the study is that domestic factors play critical roles. In particular, the formation of a majority government with no ideological opposition to decentralization and the recognition of policy failure on the part of the bureaucrats at the SPO provided a domestic context conducive to domestic change when confronted with EU requirements. In this domestic context, the EU requirements for participation and programming served to fulfil both the political interests of the government in power and the gaps in know-how in the bureaucracy for effective regional planning.

The EU's significance stems from triggering, at the right time, 'thin learning' on the part of political actors in power on the one hand and accelerating the process of policy learning, which has already been under way by domestic bureaucrats on the other. The latter involves a process of 'thick-learning that is modifying the bureaucrats' preferences regarding the system of regional development governance. The effect has been the development of some features of multi-level governance, even if this has to date only very gently pushed Turkey in the direction of becoming a more compound polity.

Notes

1. This study draws on insights gained from in-depth interviews conducted with 17 elite-level actors who represent national government officials, EU officials and subnational officials most relevant to the area of cohesion policy. Seventeen interviewees include: 10 bureaucrats at the SPO and two officials at the EUSG in Ankara (Winter 2008 and 2009); two EU officials at the Commission Delegation in Ankara (Winter 2008) and three representatives from three development agencies (Istanbul, Izmir and Cukurova Development Agencies) (Summer 2009). References to interviews in the main text of the discussion represent points of view on which there is agreement among the interviewees. Interviews were conducted on the basis of individual anonymity and confidentiality. The main questions during the interviews addressed the following: Who are the key actors and key institutions at different stages of the decision-making and implementation processes? What kind of changes can be observed in terms of participation in comparison to the previous period? Which actors play key roles? What is the degree of participation and influence in relation to other actors? What are the reasons for their high or low degree of influence? What kind of evidence is there to show the degree of influence exerted? What explains the observed changes? What are the incentives for change? Does learning play a role in change? What kind of a role does the EU play? How important is the role of the EU in comparison to other actors in domestic change?
2. It should be noted that the Regional Development Administration for the Southeast Anatolia Project (GAP), which is the only one of its kind in Turkey, is a deconcentrated arm of government for coordinating what is mostly perceived as public works investments by government institutions in this region.
3. Turkey started accession negotiations in 2005, and so far, negotiations opened in 11 *acquis* chapters not including regional policy.
4. For an explanation of the NUTS classification system, see Bache (2010).
5. This is according to the author's own calculations. Also see CEC (2007b, 2).
6. Here, we draw on the two types of multi-level governance developed by Marks and Hooghe (2004; see also Bache 2010). Type I multi-level governance describes system-wide governing arrangements in which the dispersion of authority is restricted to a limited number of clearly defined, non-overlapping jurisdictions at a limited number of territorial levels, each

of which has responsibility for a 'bundle' of functions. By contrast, Type II multi-level governance describes governing arrangements in which the jurisdiction of authority is task-specific, where jurisdictions operate at numerous territorial levels and may be overlapping.

7. Of the total amount of regional development grants, between 87% and 100% were contracted (contracts signed with beneficiaries). See http://www.dpt.gov.tr/bgyu/abbp/Programlar/DAKP_bilgi.html.

8. Also see minutes of the sectoral monitoring committee meetings at: http://ipa.stb.gov.tr/en/Home.aspx (accessed in 2009).

9. Draft Framework Law on Public Administration available at http://www.tbmm.gov.tr (accessed in 2003).

10. Turkey's regional disparities are much more marked than in any country of the EU. In 2001, per capita income in the five poorest NUTS 2 regions was between 33% and 53% of national average while income in the five richest regions varied between 127% and 190% of national average (CEC 2007a).

References

Bache, I. 2010. Europeanization and multi-level governance: EU cohesion policy and pre-accession aid in Southeast Europe. *Southeast European and Black Sea Studies* 10, no. 1: 1–12.

CEC. 2007a. *Commission Decision on a Multi-annual Indicative Planning Document (MIPD) 2007–2009 for Turkey.* http://ec.europa.eu/enlargement/pdf/mipd_turkey_2007_2009_en.pdf.

CEC. 2007b. Communication from the commission to the council and the European Parliament. Instrument for Pre-Accession Assistance (IPA). Multi-annual Indicative Financial Framework for 2009–2011. November 6, COM(2007) 689 final, Brussels.

Cizre-Sakallıoğlu, Ü. 1997. The anatomy of the Turkish military's political economy. *Comparative Politics* 29, no. 2: 57–74.

Cizre-Sakallıoğlu, Ü., and E. Yeldan. 2000. Politics, society and financial liberalization: Turkey in the 1990s. *Development and Change* 31, no. 2: 481–508.

Danielson, M., and R. Keleş. 1985. *The politics of rapid modernisation: Government and growth in modern Turkey.* New York: Holmes and Meier.

GAP. 2002. *Güneydoğu Anadolu Projesi Bölge Kalkınma Planı* [Southeast Anatolia Project Regional Development Plan]. Vol. 1. Ankara: GAP.

Güler, B.A. 1998. *Yerel Yönetimler: Liberal Açıklamalara Eleştirel Yaklaşım* [Local governments: A critical approach to liberal explanations]. Ankara: Türkiye ve Orta Doğu Amme İdaresi Enstitüsü.

Güler, B.A. 2003. İkinci Dalga: Siyasal ve Yonetsel Liberalizasyon. Kamu Yönetimi Temel Kanunu [Second wave: Political and administrative liberalization. Basic law on public management]. Special issue, *A.Ü. SBF GETA Tartışma Metinleri* (Ankara University, Faculty of Political Science, GETA Working Paper Series), no. 59, November: 1–34.

Heper, M. 1990. The state, political party and society in post-1983 Turkey. *Government and Opposition* 25, no. 3: 321–34.

Heper, M. 1991. Transitions to democracy reconsidered: A historical perspective. In *Comparative political dynamics: Global research perspectives*, ed. D.A. Rustow and K.P. Erickson, 192–210. New York: Harper Collins.

HRD-OP. 2007. *Human Resources Development Operational Programme* (CCI No. 2007 TR 05 I PO 001). Ankara: Ministry of Labour and Social Security.

Kalaycıoğlu, E. 2001. Turkish democracy: Patronage versus governance. *Turkish Studies* 2, no. 1: 54–70.

Marks, G., and L. Hooghe. 2004. Contrasting visions of multi-level governance. In *Multi-level governance*, ed. I. Bache and M. Flinders, 15–30. Oxford: Oxford University Press.

OJ. 2006. Official Journal. No. 26074. Ankara, February 8 [in Turkish].

OJ. 2008a. Official Journal. Regulation on project and activity support in development agencies. No. 27048. Ankara, November 8 [in Turkish].

OJ. 2008b. Official Journal. No. 26796. Ankara, February 23 [in Turkish].

RCOP. 2007. *Regional competitiveness operational programme* (CCI no. 2007 TR 16 I PO 003). Ankara: Ministry of Industry and Trade.

Şengül, T. 2003. Yerel Devlet Sorunu ve Yerel Devletin Dönüşümünde Yeni Eğilimler [The question of local state and new trends in the transformation of the local state]. *Praksis* 9: 183–220.

SPO (State Planning Organization). 2000. 8. *Beş Yıllık Kalkınma Planı. Bölgesel Gelişme Özel İhtisas Komisyonu Raporu* [8th Five year development plan. Regional Development Special Expert Commission Report]. Ankara: SPO.

SPO. 2007. *AB Bölgesel Programları Dairesi Bilgi Notu* [Information note by EU regional programmes department]. Ankara: SPO.

Sunar, İ. 1994. The politics of state interventionism in 'populist' Egypt and Turkey. In *Developmentalism and beyond: Society and politics in Egypt and Turkey*, ed. A. Öncü, Ç. Keyder, and S.E. İbrahim, 94–107. Cairo: The American University in Cairo.

Tekeli, İ. 1972. *Bölge Planlama Üzerine* [On regional planning]. İstanbul: Istanbul Technical University Press.

Tekeli, İ. 2007. *Türkiye'de bölgesel eşitsizlik ve bölge planlama yazıları* [Regional disparities and regional planning in Turkey]. İstanbul: History Foundation.

Waldner, D. 1999. *State building and late development.* Ithaca, NY: Cornell University Press.

Building multi-level governance in Southeast Europe?

Ian Bache

Department of Politics, University of Sheffield, Sheffield, UK

Drawing on the contributions to this volume, this concluding analysis reflects on the extent to which European Union (EU) cohesion policy and related pre-accession instruments are contributing to the development of more compound polities in Southeast Europe and, specifically, promoting multi-level governance. It argues that these EU policies have created more compound polities but that system-wide multi-level governance remains weak in the case study states and central governments remain prominent. However, there are interesting and potentially important developments in relation to particular features of multi-level governance, not least in states whose engagement with the EU in this sphere is relatively new. As such, a large part of this story appears yet to unfold.

Introduction

Drawing on the contributions to this volume, this concluding analysis reflects on the extent to which European Union (EU) cohesion policy and related pre-accession instruments are contributing to the development of more compound polities in Southeast Europe and, specifically, promoting multi-level governance. In doing so, it begins by recapitulating the main requirements that relate to our research on multi-level governance. Beyond this, we distinguish between the effects on different types of multi-level governance and variations across vertical and horizontal dimensions, before considering the main causes of and constraints on change and whether there is a process of Europeanization evident.

We conclude that, in broad terms, engaging with EU cohesion policies and pre-accession aid has made the simple polities of Southeast Europe more compound. However, system-wide multi-level governance remains weak in the case study states and central governments remain prominent. Yet, there are interesting and potentially important developments in relation to particular features of multi-level governance, not least in states whose engagement with the EU in this sphere is relatively new. As such, a large part of this story appears yet to unfold.

The requirements of EU cohesion policy and related pre-accession instruments

The opening contribution of this volume sets out the requirements of EU cohesion policy with relevance for multi-level governance, namely regionalization, partnership and programming. These principles have been a consistent feature of structural policy since 1989. Before the introduction of the consolidated Instrument for Pre-Accession Assistance (IPA) in 2007, the pre-accession instruments did not generally emphasize these requirements, although decentralization and partnership were features in some instances. From 2007, Component 3 (regional development) and Component 4 (human resources development) of IPA mirrored structural fund requirements to prepare EU applicants more effectively for managing these funds post-accession. As the opening contribution suggests, analysing the governance effects of cohesion policy and related pre-accession instruments in Southeast Europe requires cognizance of the variations in the requirements of different policies and instruments, of how key principles have evolved over time and of how the requirements have been applied differently by the Commission in different contexts (Bache 2010a).

The purpose of this volume has been to examine the governance effects of these requirements in seven Southeast European states: Greece, Slovenia, Bulgaria, Romania, Croatia, F.Y.R. Macedonia and Turkey. These states each fit into the 'simple' category of states defined by Schmidt (2006), in which power and influence are traditionally more concentrated in a single level and mode of governance. This categorization of states contrasts with that of compound polities, in which power and influence are diffused through multiple levels and modes of governance. On the continuum between simple and compound polities, the EU is very much at the compound end, and its requirements for cohesion policy tend to reflect this position and set of preferences. While there are important variations among our case study states, the overall effect of engaging with the EU in this policy sphere has been to pull states more towards the compound polity end of the spectrum. However, the extent to which multi-level governance is evident varies across types (I and II), dimensions (vertical and horizontal) and territories.

Towards multi-level governance?

It is clear from the contributions here that EU cohesion policy and related pre-accession instruments have had significant effects on both the vertical and horizontal dimensions of multi-level governance across Southeast Europe. This has spawned Type II bodies of various kinds in all states – agencies, working groups, task forces and numerous partnership bodies at both national and subnational levels. However, the effects on Type I multi-level governance are less significant. While new bodies have been created at regional level in most of the case study states, these remain task-specific and have not developed into multi-purpose organizations with a prominent place in the system-wide governance architecture. Such developments would require powerful domestic imperatives to build on the nascent institutions created by the EU, which have been absent to date in our case study states. Despite this, EU cohesion policy and related instruments have had a perceptible effect on the dynamic between territorial levels of governance in Southeast Europe: the vertical dimension of multi-level governance.

The vertical dimension

In all of the countries discussed, a regional tier of some description and status has been created for the administration of EU funds, although the importance of these 'regions' and the resources allocated to them varies considerably. In some cases, they exist purely as statistical regions, and central government officials administer the funds. In others, regional development agencies (RDAs) have been established, overseen by appointed regional councils. In addition to creating a further tier, the EU has also sought to build the capacity of existing subnational actors, although again to varying degrees in different cases and with different effects. The section below gives a flavour of some of the variations resulting from these activities.

In Greece, Andreou (2010) identifies an initial process of regionalization in response to the demands of structural policy but a later recentralization (below). Regarding Bulgaria, Yanakiev (2010) argues that the pivotal role of central government in negotiations with the Commission and in the implementation process has generally strengthened its position in the domestic arena, with cohesion policy having no significant territorial impact to date.

The situation in Romania appears more nuanced. Again, regional structures have been established to comply with EU requirements rather than through any particular domestic demand. However, the EU's activity in this and other policy areas has been seen to create a new set of opportunities for subnational actors. In Romania, 'new regional and local private actors emerged such as regional associations and county associations which opened representations in Brussels. Groups of citizens, mainly professors and journalists, started writing manifestos on regionalization and new regional political parties were created' (Dobre 2010, 68). Thus, while the new regional structures have not yet succeeded in mobilizing and aggregating regional interests, 'regional institutions have moved forward slowly and hesitatingly, building their performance and social legitimacy on the EU framework' (Dobre 2010, 68–9).

The situation in Turkey provides another variation. Like other states in the region, Turkey has a strong tradition of centralization and a concomitant concern that regionalization might endanger the unity and security of the nation. Despite this tradition, RDAs have been established at the NUTS 2 level,[1] and this has been a distinct EU effect. While RDAs have a limited role to date, their creation is seen to 'strengthen considerably' the vertical dimension of multi-level governance and 'create an opportunity for regional and local levels to exercise real influence over outcomes' (Ertugal 2010, 103). Yet, although the RDAs create a new focal point for activity at the regional level and lead to the proliferation of interactions between national and subnational levels, this is in a context where the central state remains dominant (below). Moreover, there is variation within Turkey, with RDAs only established in eight of the 24 NUTS 2 regions to date.

The Slovenian case is unusual in that in the pre-accession period, domestic actors were interested in promoting the regional tier, whereas the Commission preferred a centralized approach to administering the funds, given the relatively small size of the country and the priority of absorbing funds, so as not to delay accession. This emphasis changed post-accession when DG Regio became the lead Commission directorate and concurred with prevailing domestic opinion on the value of a regional approach. In this case, therefore, the domestic position has clearly been of paramount importance.

Croatia and F.Y.R. Macedonia, as with Slovenia, are small countries where the logic of *regional* development is less strong than in the larger states discussed above. However, partly through EU encouragement and incentivization, Croatia has seen a mobilization in subnational activity that has been stimulated partly by EU policies and support, even though the Commission's primary focus is on ensuring an effective centralized system for the administration of funds. In F.Y.R. Macedonia, the focus of the Commission remains very much on developing central capacity, although the development of subnational capacity remains part of its agenda. Moreover, eight NUTS 3 regions have been established for the purposes of implementing the regional dimension of development policy, which are overseen by regional planning councils established by local mayors.

In short, the vertical dimension of multi-level governance has generally been strengthened by EU cohesion policy and related pre-accession instruments, but the effects have been uneven. Moreover, and as we will discuss further in relation to the role and power of the state, the changes that have occurred have often been accommo-dated within or alongside other arrangements or are in relatively early stages of their development and have not posed a serious threat to the dominance of the central government. However, with the possible exception of Greece, it is likely that the full implication of these changes is yet to be fully realized and understood.

The horizontal dimension

The pressure for states to enhance horizontal participation in policy-making has increased over time for long-standing member states, with each reform of the struc-tural funds since 1989 (see Bache 2010). Greece was initially a sluggish and reluctant implementer of partnership requirements but has learned to live more easily with these requirements over time. In Slovenia, a more recent member state, the partnership principle has been implemented in accordance with the letter of EU requirements rather than the spirit. The policy process is heavily dominated by central ministries, and non-state actors express dissatisfaction with their lack of influence.

Although the partnership requirement has been relatively short term and less clearly specified in Croatia and F.Y.R. Macedonia, there have, nonetheless, been marked effects in both cases. In Croatia, there is early evidence of partnership having spread to areas of domestic policy, and in F.Y.R. Macedonia, there is an observable difference over the period of engagement with the EU in relation to the intensification of stakeholder participation. Here, the shift from applicant to candidate country status has been crucial in accelerating this process, although it is too early to say at this stage whether these changes will be sustained in the longer term and become embedded in domestic practices.

In Bulgaria, partnership again appears to be more procedural than substantive. Central government has engaged various partners from business, civil society, devel-opment agencies, etc., in the drafting of various strategic documents, and partners have participated in the monitoring committees for the National Strategic Reference Framework and operational programmes. However, 'the decision making process in the monitoring committees and similar bodies remained under the control of the state' (Yanakiev 2010, 55).

In Turkey, the horizontal dimension of multi-level governance is evident at national level through the involvement of social and economic partners in sectoral monitoring committees, but at the local level, it is seen to be very weak. As Ertugal (2010, 98) notes: 'a characteristic feature of Turkey's governing system at the local level has been the absence of coordinating mechanisms among public and local authorities'.

In Romania, subnational authorities and economic and social partners were active participants in the definition of policy for the regional operational programmes for 2007–2013. Dobre (2010) reports how, at regional level, actors met within the framework of the so-called Regional Consortiums, which are headed and coordinated by the RDAs. While these fora were seen as important in providing actors with a channel to accession decision-making, this was a relatively new development and the one whose significance had not had time to unfold.

Other governance effects

Goetz has argued that engagement with the EU limits discretion over the temporal ordering of decision-making within states: 'The national political process has to adjust firmly to decision-making rhythms and detailed calendars of supranational processes of decision-making and negotiation' (Jerneck 2000, 39, as cited in Goetz 2009, 214). There is certainly evidence here for this argument. EU cohesion policy works to the rhythm of distinct programme periods and is subject to periodic reform (since 1999, every seven years). The requirements of co-funding from domestic sources generally lead to a realignment of domestic regional policy cycles, especially where the EU contribution far outweighs domestically funded initiatives. This is the case in a number of the case studies covered here and, where regional policy is effectively new (e.g. Croatia and F.Y.R. Macedonia), it tends to be created in line with EU processes and timeframes.

In all cases, at some point or other in their engagement, the requirements of EU cohesion policy have exposed capacity deficiencies within the institutions of government. There have been acute problems in relation to capacity at subnational levels, but it is a typical feature of our cases that central capacity has also required development. In some cases, this has meant creating a new central unit or agency specifically for the purpose of handling EU funds, whereas in others, it has required the training and development of staff in an existing unit. As noted above, in many cases, the priority has been to develop central capacity first – to ensure the absorption of funds – before moving on to the local level. The development of state capacity has, on occasions, led to a redistribution of power within central government. As Yanakiev (2010) notes, in the case of Bulgaria, cohesion policy led to the rearrangement of the institutional framework within central government, and from this, the Ministry of Finance emerged as a much more influential player.

Alongside this focus on state capacity, funding has been regularly directed at developing the capacity of non-state actors to allow them to participate in the policy-making process. In this respect, EU cohesion policies have promoted the skills and knowledge base of domestic actors who are then able to apply these attributes in other policy arenas.

The role and power of the central state

A central theme of discussion on multi-level governance is the extent to which it impacts on the role and power of the central state. While emerging multi-level governance is inevitably a challenge to established governing modes and institutions, the extent to which power is redistributed as a result is an empirical question. Generally, what we find here is that the role of the state is necessarily affected by the requirements of EU cohesion policy and related instruments, but that its power is not necessarily undermined. In all of the cases studied, the central state emerges as resilient and dominant.

In relation to Greece, Andreou (2010) found that although the necessary multi-level governance structures and processes were established for the implementation of cohesion policy, the core of the pre-existing institutions, processes and policies remained unchanged. These parallel arrangements were sold as 'refinements or correctives' to existing governing arrangements.

Regarding Turkey, Ertugal found change in both the vertical and horizontal dimensions of multi-level governance through EU policies, but this had not yet undermined the role, power and authority of central state actors:

> Rather, the role of the state in regional policy and development is going through significant change as the governing context changes. Whereas previously the state proved to be ineffective in formulating and implementing a nation-wide regional plan and strategy in a highly centralized polity, the new arrangements provide the opportunity to increase state effectiveness in a policy area in which the sheer size and diversity of the country matters to a great extent. (2010, 104–5)

Similar comments are made in each of the cases covered. The power of central government has not been significantly undermined, but how it seeks to exercise power and influence has been adjusted to the demands of changing circumstances. A theme common in a number of cases is the layering of multi-level governance arrangements on top of core institutions and processes in a way that does not appreciably alter existing power dependencies between national and subnational levels. In terms of horizontal relations, ministries tend to coordinate the development of key strategic documents, chair and administer the major programme committees, and shape which actors participate at different stages of policy-making.

Explaining change: a case of Europeanization

In the opening contribution of this volume, Europeanization was defined for the purposes of this study as: 'the reorientation or reshaping of politics (and governance) in the domestic arena in ways that reflect policies, practices or preferences advanced through the EU system of governance' (Bache 2010b, 3). It is evident from the case studies that there is a process of Europeanization taking place in Southeast Europe that is either reshaping or reorienting structures and processes of governance in ways that resemble EU policies, practices and preferences, even if the changes are, in many cases, incremental and sector-specific.

Yet, Europeanization is not the only process that is promoting changes in domestic governance: other international factors also matter, but domestic processes are particularly important in both mediating the impact of EU processes and catalysing independent processes of change. An important illustration of this is how discourses of Europeanization and modernization in some states often overlap, so that the terms and the related processes become almost synonymous. In all cases, understanding the degree of Europeanization evident requires a detailed understanding of domestic politics and governance. We return to this theme below, but we begin our discussion of some of the key Europeanization themes that framed our analysis.

The notion of 'misfit'

The notion of misfit is a useful starting point for Europeanization research that focuses primarily on the top-down effects of the EU on domestic change. Fairly obviously, it points out that if there is no misfit between what the EU requires and what member/candidate states do, then there is no need for change. Beyond this, it infers that the higher is the degree of misfit, all other things being equal, the greater is the degree of pressure on the state to change. Of course, in practice, all other things are not equal, and the value of this heuristic diminishes at the level of detailed investigation.

In this vein, the distinction between simple and compound polities provides a useful point of departure for comparative analysis. However, as Schmidt (2006, 232) acknowledged, these categories are very broad, and 'micro' patterns of policy-making in a specific sector may not always conform to the 'macro' patterns of states in particular sectors because of specificities at either or both the EU and national levels. Thus, there were some counter-intuitive findings in our cases.

Slovenia, for example, was identified as the most compound polity in the collection, with a strong corporatist tradition. As such, it might reasonably be expected to adjust to the EU's partnership requirements relatively easily. Yet, in this case, the policy specifics do not fit with the particular tradition of corporatism. Slovenian tripartism is a collaboration between the state and social and economic partners in relation to defined policy areas. There was little evidence here to suggest that Slovenian central ministries were any more open to partnership with actors in other policy spheres than the national ministries studied or than those in the less corporatist polities. In this case, other factors trumped any inherent tradition towards cooperation, not least competition between ministries, which was often party political.

Moreover, the degree of adaptational pressure cannot be read off from any apparent misfit between EU requirements and domestic practices. As we have noted above, what the EU requires in practice varies independently of changes in formal requirements. And, moreover, what constitutes 'pressure' in the domestic context is heavily conditioned by the various domestic factors that are revealed through empirical research. These generally include the extent to which there are complementary and/or countervailing domestic forces present and the capacity for change.

Thus, in a case such as F.Y.R. Macedonia, the partnership requirement is not a pressure in the sense that it runs against the grain of what key domestic actors want – there are both complementary and countervailing forces. Rather, pressure exists in this case in a more practical sense of developing the necessary capacity of subnational and non-state actors in order for them to participate effectively. More generally, misfit should not be understood as an objective condition, but one that is constructed differently at different times – e.g. pre- and post-accession – and in different contexts and arenas, not least when domestic actors use one discourse in EU circles and another in the national context.

Time, timing and sequencing

As North (1990, 316) put it, 'time is the dimension in which ideas and institutions and beliefs evolve'. This argument is best illustrated here by the case of Greece, which has been subject to EU cohesion policy requirements not only longer than our other case study states but also longer than any other member state, because the concepts of partnership and regional programming were piloted in the Integrated Mediterranean Programmes in Greece in the mid-1980s (see Andreou 2010) before being incorporated into the regulations governing other structural funds from 1989. The Greek case demonstrates that change over time is neither linear nor even across different dimensions.

COHESION POLICY AND MULTI-LEVEL GOVERNANCE IN SOUTH EAST EUROPE

The most significant vertical effect in Greece was the creation of 13 administrative regions in 1989, necessary to comply with the new structural fund requirements for regional programming. Despite the strong tradition of centralization in Greece, national authorities in this still newly acceded member state were keen to comply. There was never any intention at the central level for these administrative regions to become political bodies, but this was nonetheless a novel tier of administration in the Greek system. However, it was not long before these already weak regions had been further weakened as central government assumed greater control over the planning and administration of operational programmes. As Andreou put it:

> In the first place, Greece had to comply with the new regulations and show some respon-siveness to Commission criticisms, otherwise the inflow of EU funds would have been jeopardized. On the other hand, the manifest policy failure of the first CSF [Community Support Framework] and the accumulation of experience militated for reform and for some degree of adjustment to EU norms. (2010, 24)

While the vertical dimension demonstrates an initial shift towards multi-level governance followed by a process of recentralization, in other respects, there has been evidence of 'thick' learning over time. This is manifest at the central level, in peak employer organizations and in the technical profession, and is reflected in 'increases in policy effectiveness, in the adoption and diffusion of new management techniques and in the dissemination – and even the export – of good practices' (Andreou 2010, 24).

If the case of Greece illustrates initial post-membership enthusiasm for compliance, the incentive of membership has often been seen as more important in this regard (Schimmelfennig and Sedelmeier 2005), and this was illustrated in the cases of Croatia and F.Y.R. Macedonia, in particular. Moreover, Croatia's and F.Y.R. Macedonia's position in the sequence of enlargements is important. The experience and effects of previous enlargements shape the demands, expectations and prospects of future enlargements, and the difficulties faced by the EU in coping with the enlargements of 2004 and 2007 have not improved the accession prospects of other states.

Thus, whereas Slovenia provides a good example of a state that was part of an enlargement tide with an almost irresistible momentum, once under way, Croatia and F.Y.R. Macedonia are not. There is now less political will for enlargement than a decade ago, and there is no sense, as there was with the fifth enlargement, that there was a historic opportunity that had a limited timeframe. In short, the accession pros-pect for Croatia, F.Y.R. Macedonia, Turkey and others is more open-ended than with previous enlargements, and this has an effect on both the degree of compliance required and the time available to ensure that adequate compliance is achieved. Moreover, in our policy field, the compliance requirements have become clearer and arguably tougher (through the revision of IPA) as a consequence of previous enlarge-ment experiences.

Sequencing is also important in another sense. To the extent that Croatia, F.Y.R. Macedonia and Turkey have begun to embrace notions of partnership and stake-holder participation, this is partly because they are now seen as part of a process, not just of Europeanization but also of modernization. This was not the case during the period of the Greek accession, but these notions have steadily become part of the architecture of 'modern' European governance – both for EU policies and those of member states – and EU cohesion policy has played a role in making this so (see Bache 2008).

Learning

Not unexpectedly, the nature of the learning that has taken place in the case studies is primarily 'thin' and strategic rather than 'thick' and transformative. In other words, actors have responded rationally to the external incentives – whether funding alone or connected to the membership perspective – in complying with EU requirements. Only in limited cases and spheres has learning through engagement transformed actor preferences. Here, Greece is a case in point where EU practices have been adopted in domestic policy areas (see above). This finding is not surprising because it takes time for learning of a deeper kind to take place. Despite this, there is evidence in other cases of actors genuinely embracing EU policies. In Croatia, for example, the internalization of EU practices has been seen to produce a number of collaborative initiatives at subnational level.

Of course, it is difficult to be absolutely clear that such behaviour is more than strategic. Yet, there are reasons to accept that this might be the case, not least because societies in transition are often genuinely in search of ideas and practices that have been tried and tested elsewhere and appear to have an underlying logic. The partnership principle is a case in point. While EU cohesion policy may have been at the forefront of promoting partnership as a mode of governance, it is now a prominent feature of governance throughout Europe and beyond for a range of public policies.

However, the more recent cases have also revealed something of a divide within political and administrative elites in their degree of support for EU initiatives. Often, this relates to the influx of a younger generation of civil servants who have been educated or trained in other European states and who tend to have a more Europeanized perspective. This feature (evident in Croatia and F.Y.R. Macedonia) adds another layer of complexity to EU receptivity on top of the more obvious political and institutional dynamics. It means that learning is often most likely among certain types of actors often located in ministries and agencies that are closely related to EU policies, which can then lead to an internal struggle with other actors (and organizations) over how far and how fast the EU's approach should be adopted.

Party politics

One issue that is sometimes overlooked in the Europeanization literature is the importance of party political contestation in the domestic arena in shaping outcomes. Relationships between parties have a tangible effect on the organizational arrangements relating to cohesion policy. In Slovenia, for example, the coordinating body for cohesion policy is headed by a minister without portfolio from a junior partner of the coalition government, which limits their clout within government. Slovenia also provides a good example of how party political change can contribute to volatility in the domestic processes of handling EU funds and also of how party connections can affect the degree of influence on central government of different local authorities. The F.Y.R. Macedonia case reveals how changes of governing party can lead to abrupt changes in administration, thus disrupting the implementation process and limiting the prospects for institutional learning.

Multi-level governance

While the concepts applied here have been helpful in guiding research and organizing the findings, there is scope for a more critical interrogation of the concepts of

Europeanization and multi-level governance. In particular, the application of multi-level governance has been brought into question by Stubbs (2005) who describes the concept as a 'rehashed pluralism' and suggests it might conceal more than it reveals in relation to issues of power.

This characterization assumes that multi-level governance necessarily infers a cosy consensual set of arrangements in which power is dispersed and conflict is absent. Seen this way, it is an easy target for rehashed criticisms of ideal-type pluralism, and this interpretation of multi-level governance research overlooks the various studies focusing on the resilience of entrenched asymmetries in domestic power relations in the face of exogenous pressures and incentives.

Where they emerge, patterns of multi-level governance exhibit considerable variation (see the collection by Hooghe 1996 for an illustration of varying patterns of multi-level governance on its 'home ground' of cohesion policy) and can involve conflict as well as cooperation. In my own work on the UK, I have often argued that many of the arrangements that are characterized as multi-level governance are state-dominated, and that multi-level governance can form part of state strategy (e.g. Bache 2000, 2003). More recently, Michael Kull (2007) has identified the elite tendencies within multi-level governance processes in Finland and Germany.

Yet, despite the empirical studies that have identified asymmetries, elites and conflict in multi-level governance arrangements, multi-level governance research might do more to strengthen itself against charges that it conceals more than it reveals about the nature and distribution of power. In particular, there is scope for more research on multi-level governance that places greater emphasis on: (1) the interaction between formal (and orderly) and informal (and disorderly) governance; and (2) the effects on the distribution of different power resources (e.g. political, financial, administrative, constitutional–legal, informational) between different actors and social groups.

There is also a perception that the multi-level governance concept is not a good fit with the complexities and paradoxes of 'failed', 'weak', 'authoritarian', and 'captured/clientelist' states in Southeast Europe (Stubbs 2005, 73). Further, as Andreou (2009) points out, a similar argument has been advanced in relation to understanding the effects of EU cohesion policy (i.e. because of the qualitative differences in financial and administrative capacities between established member states and the potential member states located in Southeast Europe).

Yet, as Andreou (2009, 63) suggests, it would be erroneous to dismiss the theoretical tools applied to established member states on such a distinction or 'even more problematically, by isolating the experience of a "South East Europe" that might or might not include Greece and Cyprus'. It would not take much reflection to come up with the names of a handful of long-standing states that acceded to the EU without appropriate administration of financial capacities for supporting EU regional and structural policies. Indeed, 'the main recipients of EU assistance after the reform of the structural funds (1989) were regions located in peripheral, economically backward and politically centralized member states and ... in three out of the four original "cohesion countries" – Ireland, Portugal, and Greece – a policy that was regional by name and design became predominately a *national* policy' (Andreou 2006, 241).

Further, many of the issues that we have identified in Southeast Europe in this collection – centralization, the dominance of governance arrangements by national ministries, the exclusion of certain actors from partnerships, the lack of resourcing of subnational authorities, non-governmental organizations (NGOs) and other potential partners – were common to states such as the UK in their early engagement with the structural funds. As such, what distinguishes the old and new recipients of cohesion policy tends to be the length of engagement and the extent to which this has promoted administrative maturity. Thus, 'it is highly plausible to expect a high degree of differentiation in the nature and the quality of governance across the EU states; nevertheless, it would be incorrect to assume that this differentiation follows a consistent geographic pattern' (Andreou 2009).

Conclusion

The opening contribution to this volume hypothesized that EU cohesion policy and related pre-accession aid requirements were likely to pull our case study states in a more compound direction. Beyond testing this hypothesis, our concern has been to consider specifically whether Europeanization is having effects on the system-wide architecture of the case study states (in particular through regionalization), on the proliferation of pluralistic processes (especially through partnership) or in promoting task-specific governance arrangements.

It is clear from the contributions presented that EU cohesion policy and related pre-accession aid has had the general effect of making the polities studied more compound and has promoted features of multi-level governance. However, its effects on system-wide architecture (Type I multi-level governance) is generally marginal, while the proliferation of pluralistic processes and the promotion of task-specific (Type II) governance arrangements is significantly more marked.

The EU's cohesion policy and some of its pre-accession instruments have increased and intensified interactions between actors organized at different territorial levels and from different sectors and, in some instances, shifted the nature of interdependencies between them – at least in relation to regional development policy. Overall, though – and broadly in line with the research on the EU15 and then on the EU25 – we find that despite changes instigated by the EU, national governments can generally be effective gatekeepers over the levers of power and influence in the domestic arena.

The major caveat to enter here, however, is that with the exception of Greece, the experience of engaging with the EU in this sphere is relatively recent, and institutional change tends to be gradual and incremental. Other research indicates that in the longer term, engagement with EU cohesion policies can reshape domestic preferences and lead to a more profound shift in domestic practices where domestic circumstances are conducive (Bache 2008). In other words, what we have witnessed in Southeast Europe to date has been significant, but what we observe over the next decade or so will be more telling. We have by no means reached the endpoint in relation to Europeanization in Southeast Europe and, to paraphrase Young (1998), we cannot expect the dust to settle while the currents of Europeanization continue to blow.

Acknowledgements

I would like to thank my co-editor, George Andreou, and the two anonymous referees for the journal for their helpful comments. All the usual disclaimers apply.

Note

1. NUTS refers to Nomenclature of Territorial Units for Statistics. For an explanation of the NUTS classification system, see Bache 2010.

References

Andreou, G. 2006. EU cohesion policy in Greece: Patterns of governance and Europeanization. *South European Society and Politics* 11, no. 2: 241–59.

Andreou, G. 2009. The added value of EU cohesion policy in the Greek periphery: The case of Epirus. *Southeast European and Black Sea Studies* 9, no. 1: 59–75.

Andreou, G. 2010. The domestic effects of EU cohesion policy in Greece: Islands of Europeanization in a sea of traditional practices. *Southeast European and Black Sea Studies* 10, no. 1: 13–27.

Bache, I. 2000. Government within governance: Steering economic regeneration policy networks in Yorkshire and Humberside. *Public Administration* 78, no. 3: 575–92.

Bache, I. 2003. Governing through governance: Education policy control under new labour. *Political Studies* 51, no. 2: 300–14.

Bache, I. 2008. *Europeanization and multilevel governance: Cohesion policy in the European Union and Britain.* Lanham, MD: Rowman and Littlefield.

Bache, I. 2010a. Partnership as an EU policy instrument: A *political* history. *West European Politics* 33, no. 1: 58–74.

Bache, I. 2010b. Europeanization and multi-level governance: EU cohesion policy and pre-accession aid in Southeast Europe. *Southeast European and Black Sea Studies* 10, no. 1: 1–12.

Dobre, A.M. 2010. Europeanization and new patterns of multi-level governance in Romania. *Southeast European and Black Sea Studies* 10, no. 1: 59–70.

Ertugal, E. 2010. Europeanization and multi-level governance in Turkey. *Southeast European and Black Sea Studies* 10, no. 1: 97–110.

Goetz, K. 2009. How does the EU tick? Five propositions on political time. *Journal of European Public Policy* 16, no. 2: 202–20.

Hooghe, L., ed. 1996. *Cohesion policy and European integration.* Oxford: Oxford University Press.

Kull, M. 2007. EU-multi-level governance in the making: The community initiative LEADER+ in Finland and Germany. PhD diss., University of Helsinki/Tallinn University of Technology.

North, D. 1990. *Institutions, institutional change and economic performance.* Cambridge: Cambridge University Press.

Schimmelfennig, F., and U. Sedelmeier, eds. 2005. *The Europeanization of Central and Eastern Europe.* Ithaca, NY: Cornell University Press.

Schmidt, V. 2006. *Democracy in Europe.* Oxford: Oxford University Press.

Stubbs, P. 2005. Stretching concepts too far? Multi-level governance, policy transfer and the politics of scale in Southeast Europe. *Southeast European Politics* 6, no. 2: 66–87.

Yanakiev, A. 2010. The Europeanization of Bulgarian regional policy: A case of strengthened centralization. *Southeast European and Black Sea Studies* 10, no. 1: 45–57.

Young, H. 1998. *Individual strategy and social structure: An evolutionary theory of institutions.* Princeton, NJ: Princeton University Press.

Index

acquis communautaire 5; Bulgaria 51; Croatia 78; Romania 61; Slovenia 32
aid *see* pre-accession aid
Albania: IPA 6
Andreou, George 1, 113, 115, 118, 120
ANKO: Development Company of West Macedonia 23
appropriateness: logic of 3
Association of Free Trade Unions: employee association 32

Bache, Ian 1, 4, 9
Bachtler, J. 9
Bailey, D. 9
border control 73
Börzel, T. 49
Bosnia and Herzegovina: IPA 6
Bruszt, L. 9
Bulgaria 1, 90; *acquis communautaire* 51; actual change 51–2; causes of domestic change 53–6; central government 113; centralism 46, 50; cohesion policies and instruments 50–1; Common Market 48; communism 46; conclusion 56; Constitution (1991) 46, 47; Copenhagen Criteria 48; domestic change 51; and EU 47–9; EU conditionality 52–3; evaluation of changes 52; First World War 46; foreign donors 46; governance and politics 46–7; harmonization 51; harmonization of legislation 54; introduction 45–6; ISPA 50; market economy 53; mediating formal institutions 49; Ministry of Finance 115; misfits 48, 49, 51; monitoring committees 55–6; multiple veto points 49; National Strategic Reference Framework 56, 114; NUTS 51; NUTS 2 region 52; Opinion of the European Commission 55; Partnership and Association Agreement 47; partnerships 114; Phare 48; policy goals and change 47; political and organizational culture 50; pre-requisites for change 49; regional development 55; Sapard 51; simple

polities 46; social learning model 48; unification 50; veto points 46, 49
Bulgarian Communist Party 46

capacity building: Croatia 77; FYR Macedonia 113–14
capacity deficiencies 115
Central and East European states (CEEC): reforms 48, 53; regionalization 9
centralism 29; Bulgaria 46, 50
centralization: Romania 60; Slovenia 40; Turkey 98
change 2; learning 4; sudden 4
cohesion countries 120
Cohesion Fund 6; Slovenia 32
cohesion policy: key requirements *8*; pre-accession aid 5–7; principles 6; requirements and pre-accession instruments 111–12
cohesion regions: Slovenia 36
Common Agriculture Policy 51
Common Market: Bulgaria 48; principles 47
communism 59; Bulgaria 46
Communist Party: Romania 66; Soviet Union 46
Community Assistance for Reconstruction, Development and Stabilisation (CARDS): Croatia 73; Macedonia 88
Community Support Framework (CSF) first (1989–1993): Greece 15–16, 118
Community Support Framework (CSF) second (1994–1999): Greece 16
Community Support Framework (CSF) third (2000–2006): Greece 16–17
competitiveness 72; Croatia 78; Turkey 100
compound polity 9, 112; definition 1–2; development of 111; Romania 59, 67; Slovenia 40, 117; Turkey 108
concentration principle 6
consequentiality: logic of 3
Constitution of the V Republic 72
Copenhagen Criteria: Bulgaria 48
corporatism 31, 40

119

INDEX

Phare 6; Bulgaria 48, 50; Croatia 73; FYR Macedonia 87–8; programme 50; Romania 61; Slovenia 32, 34
Pierson, P. 4
pluralism 30, 103–4, 107; rehashed 120
Poland 6, 50; gatekeepers 9; historical institutional traditions 9
policy cycles 115
policy networks model 3
politicization: FYR Macedonia 92
polity: *see also* compound polity; simple polity
polity categories 2, 59, 71
Portugal 120
practices: embedded 4
pre-accession aid: cohesion policy 5–7
pre-accession instruments: key requirements *8*
pressure 117
privatization 30
Pro Transylvania Civic Foundation 64
programme periods 115
programming 7, 112; principle 6
proportional representation 29, 31
public-private partnerships: Croatia 76; Greece 20

rationalist accounts 3–4, *4*
rationalist approach 45
recentralization: Greece 113
regional development 7, 112; Bulgaria 55
Regional Development Agencies (RDAs): Slovenia 31, 33, 38, 41; Turkey 101–8, 113
Regional Development Fund (RDF): Romania 63
regional infrastructure 73
regional institutions: Romania 113
regionalism: Romania 64, 68
regionalization 7, 111; Central and East European states 9; Greece 112; NUTS 2 region 7; Slovenia 34; Turkey 101, 107
Rhodes, R. 3
Risse, T. 49
Roman Catholic Church 30
Romania 1, 51; *acquis communautaire* 61; centralization 60; cohesion policy and pre-accession instruments 61–2; communist party 66; compound polity 59, 67; conclusion 67–9; constitution 60, 64; Decentralization law 60; democracy 66; democratic expression 60; domestic change 66–7; EU conditionality 67; governance and politics 59–61; horizontal dimension of multi-level governance 64–5; introduction 59; ISPA 61; Local Government Act 60; National Agency for Regional Development (NARD) 62; National Development Plan (NDP) 61; NUTS 62,

65, 68; partnerships 114; Phare 61; political parties 66; Regional Consortiums 65, 115; regional development councils (RDCs) 63; Regional Development Fund (RDF) 63; regional institutions 113; regionalism 64, 68; Sapard 61; twinning 61; vertical dimension of multi-level governance 62–4; veto 66, 67, 68
rural development 7
Russia 46

Sasse, G. 9, 52, 79
Schimmelfennig, F. 52–3
Schmidt, V. 2, 5, 14; compound polity 9; polity categories 2, 59, 71; simple polity 59, 93, 112
Secretariat General for EU Affairs (EUSG) 101–4, 106, 108
Sedelmeier, U. 52–3
self-government 30
self-management 86
Serbia: IPA 6
simple polity 93, 112; Bulgaria 46; definition 1–2; FYR Macedonia 93; Turkey 98, 103
simple-compound polity distinction 1–3
Single European Act (1987) 5
single loop learning *see* thin learning
Single Programming Document (SPD): Slovenia 34
Slovenia 1; *acquis communautaire* 32; centralization 40; Cohesion Fund 32; cohesion policy and pre-accession instruments 32; cohesion regions 36; compound polity 40, 117; conclusion 40–1; corporatist culture 29; EAGGF 35; environmental issues 32; European Social Fund (ESF) 35; FIFG 35; gatekeepers 9; governance and politics 30–2; Government Office for Local Self-Government and Regional Policy (GORP) 33, 37; Government Office for Structural Policies and Regional Development(GOSP) 33, 35; historical institutional traditions 9; horizontal dimension 38–40; institutional setting (1999–2008) 32–3; introduction 29–30; ISPA 32, 34; key developments (1998–2004) 33–4; key developments (2004–2006) 34–6; Law on Balanced Regional Development 32; Ljubljana 34; monitoring committees 39; National Agency for regional Development (NARD) 33; National Development Plan 33; new financial perspective (2007–2013) 36–7; NGOs 40; NSRF 36, 37, 39; NUTS 2 region 34, 36, 37, 41, 42; NUTS 3 region 31, 33, 36, 38; Objective 1 structural funding 32, 35; partnerships 114; party

For Product Safety Concerns and Information please contact our EU
representative GPSR@taylorandfrancis.com
Taylor & Francis Verlag GmbH, Kaufingerstraße 24, 80331 München, Germany

www.ingramcontent.com/pod-product-compliance
Lightning Source LLC
Chambersburg PA
CBHW080242270326
41926CB00020B/4345

9 780415 852845